ALL ABOUT ANNUITIES

ALL ABOUT ANNUITIES

Safe Investment Havens for High-Profit Returns

Gordon K. Williamson

John Wiley & Sons, Inc.

New York • Chichester • Brisbane • Toronto • Singapore

Library of Congress Cataloging-in-Publication Data:
Williamson, Gordon K.
    All about annuities : safe investment havens for high-profit
returns / by Gordon K. Williamson.
        p.   cm.
    Includes index.
    ISBN 0-471-57425-2 (alk. paper)
    1. Annuities.   2. Variable annuities.   3. Investments.   4. Rate of
return.   I. Title.
HG8790.W55   1992
368.3'7–dc20   92-14222
                                                                        CIP

Printed in the United States of America

10 9 8 7 6 5 4 3 2 1

This book is dedicated to my mom, Ann Granger Williamson, who recently passed away. It still seems like she is with us, and I hope this feeling will never end. Ann has always been an important part of my life and a tremendous influence; she will remain so until I die. She leaves behind my dad, an equally great person. I have truly been blessed by being raised by two wonderful parents. I have learned a great deal from both my mother and my father.

Preface

During 1991, investors purchased over $50 billion in fixed-rate annuities; close to $25 billion was invested in variable annuities. Over the past few years, several hundred banks have begun selling all types of annuities. Yet, for close to 40 years, educators doctors, administrators, and other types of school and hospital personnel have been contributing to annuities. What do these millions of people know that the majority of us do not?

The tens of millions of people who have been investing in annuities know the safety, consistency, and flexibility that this investment offers. As you will see in later chapters, annuities are often the perfect answer to the question, Where should I invest my money? They provide either income, growth, a combination of growth and income, or simply security. Annuities can also be a valuable estate planning tool.

No matter what your age or income, it is not too late for you to benefit from investing in annuities. Annuities can be purchased for either a short- or long-term period. They can be utilized by young and old, single investors as well as couples. The investment can be a small or large amount, a lump sum or a series of contributions. Annuities can be either part of a retirement plan or used as a general investment. Their appeal is broad: Some annuities are extremely safe and conservative, whereas others are more risky and offer potentially large returns.

In this book you will learn exactly what annuities are, who uses them, why you should be using them, the different varieties offered, and where you can turn to for additional information. This book also contains detailed track records of 20 different annuities, how they have performed, and the type of risk taken to gain those returns.

This is the first book ever written about annuities. When you have finished reading it, you will know more about annuities than any of your friends or neighbors. If you are a stockbroker, banker, financial planner, insurance agent, accountant, or any type of investment advisor, this book will provide you with a tremendous advantage over the competition.

Acknowledgments

I would like to thank three very special people: first, my agent, Julie Castiglia of Del Mar, California. Julie is the best agent I have ever had and has never stopped believing in me. Second, my co-worker, Ursel Jones; she continues to watch over me while still doing an excellent job running our offices. Third, Wendy Grau, the editor of this book. Wendy provided me with additional ideas that I believe add some nice finishing touches to the text. All three of these people have been very patient with me; I look forward to working with them on future projects.

If You Need Help

If you wish to contact the author for further information, feel free to contact him at:

> Gordon K. Williamson & Associates
> 7911 Herschel Avenue, Suite 201
> La Jolla, California 92037
> 1/800-748-5552

Contents

ALL ABOUT ANNUITIES

CHAPTER 1

What Is an Annuity?

An annuity is an *investment* you make through an insurance company. It represents a contractual relationship between you and the company. Although annuities are *offered* only by the insurance industry, they do not have anything to do with life insurance or any other type of insurance coverage. Annuities are *marketed* and sold through brokerage firms, insurance agencies, banks, savings and loan institutions, financial planners, and investment advisors.

When you purchase or invest in an annuity, the insurance company gives you certain assurances. The guarantees depend upon the *type* of annuity. There are two different types of annuities: fixed (a set rate of return) and variable (the investor chooses from a series of portfolios that range from conservative to aggressive).

Parties to an Annuity

There are always four parties to each annuity: the insurer, the contract owner, the annuitant, and the beneficiary.

The Insurer

Whether you invest in an annuity through your local bank, financial planner, brokerage firm, or anyone else who is licensed to sell annuities, the agreement is always between you and an insurance company. There are over 2,000 insurance companies in the United States; several hundred of these insurers deal in annuities.

The insurance company you choose, also known as the *insurer*, invests your money. In addition to investing your money, the company makes certain promises. These assurances and the terms of the agreement are contained in the annuity contract. The contract spells out what can and cannot be done. Items such as additional investing, withdrawals, cancellations, penalties, and guarantees are all defined in the contract.

Perhaps the best way to explain how the insurer operates is by analogy. When you invest in a bank certificate of deposit (CD), you sign an agreement. If you purchase a mutual fund, you fill out an application. These agreements and contracts are between you and the financial institution. They tell you what your rights and privileges are; they also point out what will happen if you decide not to abide by those terms. When you invest in an annuity, you enter into a similar arrangement.

The Contract Owner

The person or couple who invests in the annuity is known as the contract owner. It is their money; they decide among the different options offered. The contract owner has the right and ability to add more money, terminate the agreement, withdraw part or all of the money, or change the parties named in the contract.

The contract owner is similar to the purchaser of a mutual fund or bank CD. When you buy a mutual fund, you are the owner. You have the right to invest more money, liquidate the entire account, take some or all of the money out, and change the title of the account (its ownership).

The contract owner can be an individual, couple, trust, corporation, or partnership. The only requirement is that the owner is an adult. A minor can be the owner as long as the policy lists the minor's custodian (e.g., "Ellise Hamilton, custodian for the benefit of Timothy Hamilton").

Since the contract owner controls the investment, he and/or she can gift or will part or all of the contract to anyone or any entity at any time.

The Annuitant

The best way to understand the purpose of the annuitant is also by analogy. When you purchase life insurance, the insured party is named. The life insurance policy continues in force until the owner terminates the contract, fails to make any required premium payments, or the insured dies. Similarly, an annuity remains in force until the contract owner makes a change or the annuitant dies. Thus, the annuitant is like the insured in a life insurance policy.

The annuitant, like an insured, has no voice or control of the contract. The annuitant does not have the power to make withdrawals, deposits, change the names of the parties to the agreement, or terminate the contract. Just as when you purchase life insurance on someone else (the insured), the annuitant must also sign the annuity contract.

The person you name as the annuitant can be anyone: you, your spouse, parent, child, relative, friend, or neighbor. The only qualification is that the named annuitant is a person (i.e., *not* a living trust, corporation, partnership, etc.) currently living who is under a certain age. The maximum age of the proposed annuitant depends on the insurance company. Most companies require that the annuitant be under the age of 75 when the contract is initially signed. Other companies set a maximum age of 70 or 80. It is important to note that the contract (the investment) may still stay in force after the annuitant reaches the maximum age.

Most annuities allow the contract owner to change the annuitant at any time. The only stipulation is that the new annuitant must have been alive when the contract was originally set up.

The Beneficiary

Like a vice president of a country, the beneficiary is of little value until the death of a certain individual. In the case of an annuity, the beneficiary is waiting for the death of the annuitant. And, like the beneficiary of a life insurance policy, the beneficiary of an annuity has no voice in the control or management of the policy. The only way in which the beneficiary can prosper from an annuity is upon the death of the annuitant.

The named beneficiary(s) can be children, friends, relatives, spouses, neighbors, trusts, corporations, or partnerships. The annuity application allows for multiple beneficiary designations of varying or similar proportions (i.e., 25% to Mary Jones, 15% to Jack Jones, 10% to Edward Smith, and 50% to the Nelson Family Trust).

In the case of a married couple, it is common for the contract owner to be either one or both spouses *and* for the annuitant to be one or both spouses. This type of multiple titling is designed to protect the assets of the couple in the case of the annuitant's untimely death. After all, most couples would not want the annuity proceeds to go to a charity or child while one or both spouses were still alive.

A single person, widow, or widower will usually name himself or herself as the contract owner and annuitant while listing a loved one or entity (e.g., living trust, charity, corporation, etc.) as the beneficiary. By making such an election, the individual retains complete control and dominion over the investment during his or her lifetime. Upon the death of the annuitant (a sole individual who is also the owner in this example), the money would automatically pass to the intended heir (children, nephews, nieces, a charity, trust, etc.).

Remember, the contract owner can change the beneficiary or beneficiaries at any time; consent by the existing beneficiary(s) is not necessary.

One Person: Multiple Titles

We now know how the four parties involved in an annuity investment operate. But the same person can hold multiple titles. Thus, you could be the contract owner and beneficiary of your own contract. Or you could be the owner, annuitant, and/or beneficiary. In fact, any combination you can think of is acceptable. Keep in mind that if you choose an entity (living trust, corporation, etc.), the entity can only be the contract owner and/or beneficiary; a living individual under a certain age (not a couple) must be named as the annuitant. Also remember that the insurer is *always* an insurance company; to change insurers you must change insurance companies.

How an Annuity Works

We have learned what an annuity is and who the parties involved are. We also know that several million people own annuities. To become more familiar with annuities, let us go through an example of how an annuity is set up, its operation, and its final disposition.

Mary Smith has some money to invest and is looking at several different types of investments, including bank CDs, government bonds, mutual funds, real estate, money market accounts, and annuities. After careful consideration, she decides to invest in an annuity. Her investment counselor discusses the pros and cons of several different annuity contracts, and Mary decides to invest in the XYZ Annuity.

The advisor gives Mary a contract (application) to complete (see Figure 1.1). The contract requests the following information (the reasons for the information requested are shown in parentheses following each item): (1) the name, address, and social security number of the contract owner (the insurance company needs to know who to send the policy to and how to identify that person for income tax purposes *if a distribution is ever made*); (2) the name, address, social security number, sex, and birth date of the annuitant, if different from the contract owner (the insurer needs to know the birth date of the annuitant to make sure that this named person is under a certain age. The sex of the annuitant is important if annuitization is later chosen—a concept that will be discussed in a later chapter); (3) investment options (depending on the type of annuity, the contract owner must decide how long the money will be invested and/or how it will be invested); (4) the type of money (the insurance company needs to know if the money being invested is being rolled over from another source, a retirement plan, or is nonqualified—a regular investment); and (5) the signature of the contract owner and annuitant (if the contract owner is not also the annuitant, this second party must sign, acknowledging that he or she has been named as the "insured").

A couple of weeks after Mary has sent her completed application and check made payable to the annuity company, she will receive her contract. The contract includes a cover sheet that summarizes parts of the application and points out what type of return Mary will receive or what type of investment portfolios she chose. Depending on the type of annuity chosen, Mary may have the ability to add money, make withdrawals, or cancel the entire contract at any time, subject to some possible penalties (discussed in a later chapter). Mary also has the right to gift part or all of this investment to someone else, change the beneficiary(s), and (with

AMERICAN SKANDIA LIFE ASSURANCE CORPORATION
P.O. BOX 883
SHELTON, CONNECTICUT 06484-9932
(Send application and check to above address.)

VARIABLE ANNUITY APPLICATION
(Please Print)

1. OWNER(S)
(Joint Owners provide same information in No. 8.)

Name: _____
First   Middle   Last

Sex: ____ Date of Birth: __/__/__ SS/Tax ID: _____

Home Address: _____
Number and Street

_____
City   State   Zip

2. PROPOSED ANNUITANT
(Complete only if different from Owner.)

Name: _____
First   Middle   Last

Sex: ____ Date of Birth: __/__/__ SS/Tax ID: _____

Home Address: _____
Number and Street

_____
City   State   Zip

3. DESIGNATED BENEFICIARY(IES)
(The Owner reserves the right to change the Beneficiary(ies) unless indicated in No. 8.)

PRIMARY BENEFICIARY
Name   Indicate relationship and to whom
_____
_____
_____
_____

CONTINGENT BENEFICIARY
Name   Indicate relationship and to whom
_____
_____
_____
_____

4. CONTRACT DETAILS   Initial Premium Payment: $ _____

Type of Money: ☐ Non-qualified   ☐ 1035   ☐ Other _____

Annuity Option: If none selected annuity payouts will commence first day of the month after age 85 for 10 years or life.

5. INVESTMENT CHOICE

Sub-account Name	%	or	$	Sub-account Name	%	or	$
				TOTAL	100%		$

6. REPLACEMENT
Is this annuity intended to replace (in whole or in part) any existing life insurance or annuity? ____ Yes ____ No
If "yes" state company, amount, reason and full details. _____

7. ADDITIONAL INFORMATION
Would you like a Statement of Additional Information? ____ Yes ____ No

8. SPECIAL INSTRUCTIONS _____

9. AGREEMENT   I/we represent to the best of my/our knowledge and belief the statements made in this application are true and complete; including, under penalty of perjury, the Social Security or Tax ID numbers provided. It is indicated and agreed that the only statements which are to be construed as the basis of the contract are those contained in this application or in any amendment to this application. I/we have also received a copy of the prospectus and I/we understand that annuity payments or surrender values when based on the investment experience of the separate account are variable and not guaranteed as to dollar amount.

SIGNATURES   Owner(s): _____   Proposed Annuitant: _____

Dated at: _____   on: __/__/__   (if different from Owner)
City   State

Signature and Number of Agent: _____   Name of Agency or Firm: _____

Address of Firm: _____
Number and Street   City   State   Zip

AGENT TO COMPLETE
Do you have any reason to believe that the contract applied for is to replace existing annuities or insurance? ____ Yes ____ No

AAA-09-88

FIGURE 1.1 **Contract Application.** (Reprinted by permission of American Skandia Life Assurance Corporation.)

many companies) change the name of the annuitant. Remember, this is Mary's money and she has quite a bit of control over what happens to it.

You now know most of the terminology and how easy it is to invest in an annuity. The next chapter points out the different investment options available—options that *you* choose.

Commonly Asked Questions

Are there any guarantees to my annuity investment?

When you purchase a fixed-rate annuity, you enter into a contract with a life insurance company—you agree to pay the premium (the "price" of your annuity) and the company agrees to provide the following benefits:

Guaranteed return of your principal. The insurance company guarantees that you will never get back less than what you have paid in. Your principal is always safe.

Guaranteed interest, which compounds tax deferred. Interest rates are guaranteed for periods of up to 10 years, and you pay no taxes on interest earned until it is withdrawn. With tax-deferred growth, your money grows faster.

Guaranteed income. If you so choose, the insurance company will agree to pay you an income you can never outlive.

Guaranteed death benefit. If you die before annuity payments begin, the company will guarantee a payment to your beneficiary.

Can I invest my annuity money in different ways?

Fixed-rate and variable annuities have two stages: the accumulation period and the payout period. The accumulation period begins as soon as you invest. You invest with one large payment if you select a single-premium deferred annuity. Or you make one or more payments of various amounts to a flexible-premium deferred annuity. Once you make a payment, your money begins to accumulate tax-deferred earnings.

Are annuities a new type of investment?

No. Annuities have been available in the United States for over 100 years. They have been available in other countries for several hundred years.

Are annuities a risky investment?

Like any other type of investment, annuities can be misused or improperly sold by an advertisement or advisor. Equally important, just like mutual funds and bank CDs, some annuities represent a bad value or have demonstrated poor performance in the past. This book will help you sort out the bad from the good.

Why should I purchase an annuity?

There are several good reasons:

1. As a safe vehicle for your money
2. For tax-deferred growth of earnings
3. To ensure that your resources last as long as you need them.

CHAPTER 2

The Different Types of Annuities

There are two ways to define annuity types: according to (1) how soon you start receiving income, and (2) how the money is invested. *When* the insurance company starts sending you checks depends on whether you choose an immediate annuity or deferred annuity. *How* the money is invested is determined by selecting either a fixed-rate or variable annuity. This chapter first discusses the income aspect of annuities and then moves on to the investment options.

Income from Annuities

Immediate Annuities: When You Need Money Now

If you purchase an immediate annuity, the insurance company will start sending you checks right away. Immediate annuities are designed for individuals or couples who rely on receiving a specific amount of money. That money may be the person's or couple's sole source of income or merely a supplement to other incoming monies.

Checks can be sent monthly, quarterly, or annually. The amount of each check will not fluctuate; the specific dollar amount of the checks, however, will depend on your total annuity investment.

Investing in an annuity should be viewed as if you were purchasing any investment; hopefully, you will do some shopping before you make a commitment. For example, when you invest in a bank certificate of deposit, one of the things you are looking for is the highest rate of return. When shopping for an annuity, part of your decision about which company to use should depend on how much money the company is willing to send you each month. Thus, when you or your advisor are comparing annuities, one of the questions you should ask is, "OK annuity XYZ, if I give you $10,000, how much will you send me each month for the rest of my life and/or the next 5, 10, 20, 30 years?" Once the insurance company gives you a specific quote, such as, "We will send you $374 each month for the next five years," have your advisor contact several other companies and find out what *they* will offer. The difference is the rate of return that each company is willing to offer.

Like any other type of investment, product, or service, some companies are more competitive than others. It pays to do some homework and find out who will give you the best possible deal.

Some investors want income on a regular basis for a specific period of time. This period may range anywhere from just a few years to the lifetime of one or two people. Certain annuities may offer handsome payments for a specific time frame (e.g., five years) but are not competitive if income for a lifetime is needed. Once you decide how long you want to receive an income stream, the task of comparing one company against another becomes much easier.

All other things being equal, the longer the time frame you choose, the less income you will receive per period (month, quarter, or year). Thus, someone who has $50,000 and wants an immediate annuity structured for monthly payments for a 10-year period will get larger monthly checks than someone who has the same amount of money to invest but is looking for monthly income for life (assuming his or her life expectancy is greater than 10 years).

Deferred Annuities: When You Want to Save Money

Most people who purchase an annuity do so because they want their money to grow. These people may or may never need an income stream. They are attracted to deferred annuities because this type of annuity provides them with the flexibility of growth for a short or long period of time, and later, if they choose, they can receive income from the annuity either through sporadic or scheduled withdrawals.

Investors who purchase bank certificates of deposit (CDs) do so because they want the interest income or because they plan on rolling over the CD and the interest upon maturity into another CD or investment. Deferred annuities can be structured in a similar fashion. The owner of the annuity can request that a certain amount of income be sent to him or her annually and the rest be reinvested. Or, as in most cases, the owner of the annuity simply has the principal and any earned interest and/or growth reinvested automatically.

The deferral process can offer a great deal of flexibility. Besides automatic reinvesting, the contract owner also has the ability, subject to possible costs, to terminate the investment or simply withdraw part of the principal.

Fixed-Rate Annuities: When You Want Guarantees

After determining if, how, and when income and/or principal is to be received, you must also determine how your money is going to be invested or reinvested. A fixed-rate annuity provides the contract owner with a guaranteed rate of return; this is very similar in concept to a bank CD.

When you purchase a CD from a financial institution, the amount of interest you receive or are credited depends on how long you are willing to commit your money and what institution you deposit it with. A fixed-rate annuity operates in the same way. Just like banks, some insurance companies offer higher rates than others. And some insurers offer fixed-rate annuities with different maturities.

The most common maturities for annuities are one, three, or five years. When you invest in a CD, the rate of return is usually locked in for a specific period of time. The same thing is true for a fixed-rate annuity: Your rate of return is *guaranteed* for the contracted period. You receive this rate whether or not the stock market goes up, interest rates go down, or the insurance company has a profitable or losing year.

Usually when you invest in a fixed-rate annuity, the longer the commitment, the higher the interest rate. The interest credited can either be sent annually or reinvested so you have a larger amount earning interest, a concept known as *compound interest* (interest earning interest).

Fixed-rate annuities are most popular with people who want assurances about the safety of their principal. These people also want to know exactly what they can expect in interest on their money. Fixed-rate annuities, since they provide guarantees regarding principal and rate of return, are ideal investment candidates for conservative investors or anyone who wants to know exactly what he or she will have at the end of a specific period of time.

Fixed-rate annuities are not just for the timid or cautious. They can provide a great stabilizing force for moderate or aggressive investors who need some balance in their overall portfolio. No matter what happens to real estate, stocks, bonds, gold, or mutual funds, all investors in fixed-rate annuities know that at least one part of their holdings is safe, secure, and *guaranteed*.

Variable Annuities: When You Want Investment Flexibility

Not every individual or couple wants a set rate of return. After all, if someone guarantees you a "floor," the "ceiling" is probably not far away. Variable annuities offer an alternative to those investments that pay a set rate of return. When you invest in a variable annuity you are, in a sense, captain of your own ship. Investing in a variable annuity is similar to investing in a mutual fund family.

An investment in a mutual fund family allows you to decide which fund or series of funds to invest in *within* the fund family. If you invest your money with the ABC mutual fund family, chances are you have several different options. There might be an ABC aggressive growth fund, an ABC government bond fund, an ABC money market fund, an ABC gold fund, an ABC high-yield fund, and/or an ABC international fund. The array of funds gives you a great deal of choice, but it also creates a burden: Do you invest in stocks, bonds, or money market instruments; or do you put some money in a couple of these funds and the majority in a favored choice? The mutual fund group will not tell you where to invest your money.

A variable annuity is just like a mutual fund family. The insurance company that offers this type of annuity does not tell you how to invest your money. The company does not share in any profits you make, and it will not absorb any of your losses. The same thing is true when you buy a stock, bond, or mutual fund. If that security goes up 35% in one year, you get to keep the entire gain. On the other hand, if that same investment falls by 20%, no one comes to your rescue.

Chapter 1 ended with an example of Mary Smith investing in an annuity. The illustration explained the different parts of the application that Mary needed to complete. If Mary were investing in a *variable* annuity, she would also have to decide where and how much of her money would go to the different investment options.

For example, if Mary had $40,000 to invest, she might opt for the following: $7,000 in a money market portfolio, $13,000 in a growth and income position, $10,000 in a government securities account, and $10,000 in international equities. Mary's only limitation is the amount of money she is willing to put in any one position (she could put it all in one specific portfolio) and, of course, the investment options that the variable annuity offers. If she were investing in the ABC mutual fund family and this group did not offer a gold fund, she could not invest in metals. She would either have to look at other mutual fund groups or set aside some money and go into a second fund family. The same thing is true with a variable annuity: You are limited by the investment choices offered by *that* company. If you do not like all of the choices, choose a different insurer.

The type of annuity selected, fixed or variable, depends on the features the investor is looking for. Those who want a set rate of return and the satisfaction of knowing their principal can never erode will opt for a fixed-rate annuity. The investor who realizes that gains and losses may occur but wants investment flexibility to move monies among a family of funds will be attracted to a variable annuity.

Which Annuity Is Best?

Both fixed-rate and variable annuities are popular. Literally billions of dollars are invested in each type of annuity every year. The type of annuity you invest in should depend on the following factors:

(1) your time horizon, (2) any existing investments you already own, (3) your goals and objectives, and (4) your risk tolerance level.

Time Horizon

The longer you are willing to live with an investment, the more you should concentrate on equity instruments. The most common is stock. Over time, common stocks or equities perform better than other assets. Debt instruments are those investments in which you have loaned someone else the use of your money. The most common example of a debt obligation is a bond.

If your time horizon for investing is only one or two years, then fixed-rate annuities are probably your best choice. Only a somewhat optimistic or aggressive contract owner, looking at a commitment of two years or less, would choose a variable annuity and then select one or more stock or long-term bond portfolios. The average investor should only consider variable annuities if he or she is looking at a time horizon of three or more years.

For example, look at the generic categories of investments that have done well over long periods of time. A time frame of 20 years or more is recommended. Your investment horizon may be a fraction of this, but keep in mind two points: (1) Twenty years includes good as well as bad times, and (2) bad results cannot be hidden when studying the long term. Even the investor looking at a one- or two-year holding period should ask, "Do I want something that does phenomenally once in every five years, or do I want something that has a very good return in eight or nine out of every ten years?" Unless you are a gambler, the answer is obvious.

Equity has outperformed debt. The longer the time frame reviewed, the better equity vehicles look. Stocks have outperformed bonds in every decade. Would you rather have lent Henry Ford or Stephen Jobs (Apple computers) the money to start their companies, or would you rather have given them money in return for a piece of the action?

A retired couple in their sixties should realize that one or both of them will live at least 15 more years. Since this is the case, and we know that equities have almost always outperformed bonds when looking at a 10-year or longer horizon, equities should be the primary choice.

The conservative investor may say that stocks are too risky. The day-to-day or year-to-year volatility of equities can be disturbing. However, it is also true that the medium- and long-term effects of inflation and the resulting diminished purchasing power is even more devastating. With an equity, there is a better than 50-50 chance that your investment will increase in value. In contrast, it is unlikely that the cost of goods and services will decrease during the next 1, 3, 5, or 10 years.

Existing Portfolio

If your current investments are mostly comprised of debt instruments, then you should view equity options (growth, growth and income, international stocks, metals, aggressive growth) within a variable annuity as serious candidates. Conversely, if most of your holdings are in equity vehicles, such as stocks or real estate, then you should consider fixed-rate or one or more of the debt portfolio options (i.e., government bonds, money market, guaranteed account, high yield) within a variable annuity.

One of the fundamentals of successful investing has always been diversification. No matter how good the debt or equity market looks, no matter how positive or negative the press or financial gurus appear, the marketplace can always change suddenly. Therefore, you do not want to have all of your assets in any one type of portfolio. As an investor, your concern is not only maximizing returns, but also being able to sleep at night.

Goals and Objectives

Typical goals of investors include to "retire comfortably," "send a child through college," or "buy a house within a few years." Your personal goals may be more or less lofty and/or complex than these. But whatever your goals are, it is important to turn them into dollar objectives. That is, if your goal is to retire comfortably, your definition of *comfortably* may mean that you need investments that can generate $1,000 a month, or you may need at least $15,000 every two weeks.

Once you know your existing holdings and the dollar amount you need, then you can easily calculate how to attain that figure (e.g., if you assume that you can safely get a 9% return on an investment and your objective is $54,000 per year, then you will need a nest egg of approximately $600,000 averaging a 9% yield annually).

If you have reviewed your goals (e.g., to retire comfortably), objectives (e.g., to end up with a lump sum of $600,000 earning 9% each year to result in a retirement income of $54,000 annually), and existing holdings ("I have $93,000 worth of investments now"), it becomes relatively easy to see what types of investments you should focus on. If the hypothetical $93,000 must grow to $600,000 in a dozen years or less, then it is almost certain that equities (one or more of the moderate or aggressive variable annuity options) must be used. If time is on your side and the $93,000 can grow to the needed $600,000 over 25 to 30 years, then you can be conservative and use fixed-rate annuities or one of the safer options offered within a variable annuity (a money market portfolio, government securities, etc.).

Risk Tolerance Level

Talking about debt versus equity instruments or how XYZ averaged 23% over each of the past 10 years is fine, but if you cannot live with the investment because of its volatility or perceived risk, then you should not be in that type of investment.

If you are not sure what your risk level is, several financial institutions, such as brokerage firms and mutual fund groups, offer quizzes that you can take and score yourself. Or, you may want to take the quiz presented in Figure 2.1. Your point total will give you a strong sense of what type of investor you are (the point scores and what they indicate immediately follow the quiz).

Commonly Asked Questions

How do I choose which type of annuity is best for me?

Your first decision is whether or not you want a guarantee (fixed-rate annuity) or flexibility (variable annuity). If you decide that you want a set rate of return, look at Chapter 14, which discusses some of the highest-yielding contracts. If you want the chance of doing much better, look at Chapter 15, which provides performance figures for a wide range of portfolios (growth, bonds, international, etc.).

A. "I invest for the long term, 5 to 10 years or more. The final result is more important than daily, monthly, or annual fluctuations in value." (1) Totally disagree; (2) Willing to accept some volatility, but not loss of principal; (3) Could accept a moderate amount of yearly fluctuation in return for a good *total* return; (4) Would accept an *occasional* negative year if the final results were good; (5) Agree.

B. Rank the importance of current income. (1) Critical, the exact amount must be known; (2) Important, but I am willing to have the amount vary each period; (3) Fairly important, but other aspects of investing are also of concern; (4) Only a modest amount of income is needed; (5) Current income is unimportant.

C. Rank the amount of loss you could tolerate in a single *quarter*. (1) None; (2) A little, but over a year's time, the total value of the investment should not decline; (3) Consistency of total return is more important than trying to get big gains; (4) One or two quarters of negative returns is the price you must pay when looking at the total picture; (5) Unimportant.

D. Rank the importance of beating inflation. (1) Factors such as preservation of principal and current income are much more important; (2) I am willing to have only a little variance in my returns, *on a quarterly basis only*, in order to have at least a partial hedge against inflation; (3) I could accept some annual volatility in order to offset inflation; (4) I consider inflation to be important but have mixed feelings about how much volatility I could accept from one year to the next; (5) The long-term effects of inflation are devastating, and no one should ignore them.

E. Rank the importance of beating the stock market over any given two- to three-year period. (1) Irrelevant; (2) A small concern; (3) Fairly important; (4) Very important; (5) Absolutely critical.

Add up your score from questions A through E. Your risk, as defined by your total point score, is as follows: 0–5 points = extremely conservative; 5–10 points = somewhat conservative; 10–15 points = moderate; 15–20 points = somewhat aggressive; 20–25 points = very aggressive.

FIGURE 2.1 **Test for Determining Your Risk Level.**

How much money should I invest in an annuity?

The answer to this question depends partly on your risk level, how your money is currently invested, and your time horizon. This chapter has helped you think about setting goals and objectives. Chapter 13 will show you how annuities fit in as part of an overall financial plan. However, like anything else in life, the answer to this question also depends on your comfort level and what "feels right" to you.

Is there an exact way to determine risk?

No. There are several different tests to help investors determine their risk profile, but there is not one that clearly stands above the others. Defining risk in precise terms is almost like trying to find a definition of *love* that everyone agrees on. The quiz included in this chapter will give you a good idea of your risk level. By reading other chapters in this book, you will learn more about what can be expected, for better or worse, at different risk levels.

Can I hedge my bets and invest in two annuities, a fixed and a variable?

You could, but probably you would not want to. It's easier to structure a variable annuity in this way by diversifying among several different subaccounts. Also, many companies offer a "hybrid annuity"—part fixed, part variable.

CHAPTER 3

The Advantages of Annuity Investing

There are positive aspects to every investment. But this does not mean that every investment is right for everybody. *All* investments also have disadvantages; there is no perfect choice. This chapter discusses the many different advantages of owning an annuity. The following chapter details the disadvantages.

Annuities, which have been available for over 100 years, provide more features than virtually any other investment. Investors can rely on the safety of the insurance industry, with its mandated reserve requirements, financial clout, and reliance on outside rating agencies. Some of the better traits of annuities include tax-deferred growth, tax-free exchanges, performance, professional management, no commission charge to the client, withdrawal options, a guaranteed death benefit, and avoidance of probate.

Safety

No one has ever lost a dime in a fixed-rate annuity. The safety record of this conservative investment vehicle is unequaled.

When you purchase a fixed-rate annuity, your principal is guaranteed every day. You can terminate the contract after being in it for only a day, month, year, or decade and always be assured that your contribution(s) is intact. There are very few investments which can use the phrase "principal guaranteed at all times." In fact, the

19

only other types of investments that can legitimately make this claim are accounts of up to $100,000 at financial institutions insured by the Federal Deposit Insurance Corporation (FDIC) and certain types of insurance contracts.

United States government securities, such as T-bills and T-bonds, are only guaranteed for face value if they are held until maturity. It is likely that you can purchase a Treasury bill today and sell it tomorrow or next week for less than you paid for it. Long-term securities, such as government bonds that mature in 20 to 30 years, can literally lose half of their value or more within a few years if interest rates increase steadily. This is what happened to bond buyers in the mid-1970s who later sold their long-term obligations during the early 1980s. However, if you hold a government security until its maturity, face value and interest are guaranteed.

Not only is your principal in a fixed-rate annuity guaranteed *at all times*, the *interest rate* received or credited to your account is also guaranteed. The interest rate is guaranteed for a specific period of time; depending on the contract you choose, the locked-in rate of return may be for one, three, five, seven, or ten years.

Notice that this discussion of safety deals only with fixed-rate annuities. The value of a variable annuity can fluctuate daily. Principal is not guaranteed on a day-to-day basis; it is secured via the guaranteed death benefit. Furthermore, the rate of return in a variable annuity is not guaranteed; the one exception is if you opt for the fixed-rate subaccount (similar to locking in a CD rate).

You may wonder why fixed-rate annuities have such strong guarantees and variable annuities do not. Keep in mind that in a variable annuity you decide which type of portfolio(s) to go into and with what dollar amount(s). And, just like mutual funds, real estate, and individual stocks or bonds, you have the potential of making or losing a modest or large amount of money.

Reserve Requirements

When you deposit a dollar in a bank account, the bank, by law, must keep a certain amount on reserve. That amount depends on the type of account but ranges from zero to 10 cents on the dollar.

When you purchase a fixed-rate annuity, the insurance company, by law, must set aside *over* a dollar in reserves. The insurer can only use these excess reserves to settle the withdrawals and redemptions of annuity owners. The money cannot be used to settle insurance claims, pay overhead, settle bad debts, or take care of any other nonrelated annuity item.

People often wonder *where* the insurer gets the excess monies from to supplement annuity deposits for reserve purposes. The answer is, from other profit centers. Conceptually, annuity business represents the smallest source of revenue for the insurance industry. Insurers generally derive much more income from selling life insurance and other forms of insurance.

In addition, most states require that any insurer doing business in the state must become part of the legal reserve pool. This pool protects annuity investors and others who purchase life insurance products or policies.

The reserve pool operates in a straightforward manner. If an insurance company goes out of business, the remaining insurers must assume the liabilities and obligations of the now defunct insurer. The liability assumed by any one insurance company depends on how much business it does in that particular state. If insurance company LMN sells 2% of all insurance and annuities issued in that state, then LMN must accept 2% of any bankrupt insurer's obligations.

If your state has a legal reserve system, it may be useful to find out how it works. The system and its extent of coverage can vary from state to state. Nevertheless, if an insurance company wishes to do business in a state that has such a reserve, it must join the pool. The state insurance commissioner will ban from the state insurers who do not join such systems.

Financial Clout

There are over 2,000 different life insurance companies in the United States. Collectively, these companies own, control, or manage more assets than all of the banks in the world combined. The insurance industry of North America owns, controls, or manages more assets than all of the oil companies in the world combined.

During the Great Depression, it was not the U.S. government that bailed out the banking industry—it was U.S. insurance companies. If there were ever a financial collapse in the United States, the insurance industry would be the second to the last entity to fold (second only to the government). This "second billing" is because the government has taxing power and, of course, the ability to print money.

If the insurance industry were to collapse, we would look back fondly at the Great Depression as a walk in the park in comparison.

Rating Services

Even though annuities have a perfect track record, some companies are safer than others. During the last few years, it has been publicized that some insurers have troubled portfolios containing large amounts of junk bonds and poor real estate holdings. Even though no one has ever lost a dime in a fixed-rate annuity, these relatively new developments have caused some alarm. For this reason, increasing numbers of people are concerned about the quality of their insurance company.

According to the oldest rating company, A.M. Best, the highest rating an insurance company can receive is A+ (superior); the second highest rating is A (excellent). Most investors should stick with companies that have an A or A+ rating. There are several dozen companies that have one of these two ratings. You do not give up anything by using a highly rated company.

Some investors like junk (high-yield) bonds because of their perceived higher return; the return is viewed as a trade-off (higher risk for the chance of getting a higher yield). This is not the case with lower-rated insurance companies and products. The investor gets very little, if any, extra return by buying a fixed-rate annuity from a lesser-rated company.

During the past few years, savvy insurance advisors have begun to look for a second rating. These advisors will only recommend annuities and insurance products to their clients if the insurer has a top rating from A. M. Best and either Moody's or Standard & Poor's.

If you are investing in a variable annuity, the rating of the insurance company is usually of little importance. When you invest in a variable annuity, your fate is not tied to the solvency of the insurer; you are not investing in the assets of the insurance company. Money invested in a variable annuity is automatically turned over to the different portfolio managers of the subaccounts. It is the performance of your subaccounts that determines the safety and return on your investment. These portfolio managers are not buying securities issued by the insurer.

Most variable annuity owners still like the idea of dealing with a highly rated company. Fortunately, potential performance or investment flexibility does not suffer by opting for a safe annuity issuer.

Tax-Deferred Growth

One of the chief reasons why tens of millions of people around the world are attracted to annuities is that money in an annuity grows and compounds on a tax-deferred basis. You do not have to indicate on your tax return the value, interest, yield, or growth of your fixed or variable annuity.

The only time you pay taxes on your annuity is if you withdraw growth or interest from the account. For example, if someone invested $20,000 in a fixed or variable annuity and the contract was now worth $55,000, the first $35,000 taken out would be taxable; the remaining $20,000 would not be taxed since it is considered a return of principal and the IRS never taxes return of principal.

The interest or growth is taxable in the year in which it is withdrawn and only on the amount actually received. Continuing the preceding example, if the investor withdrew $6,000 from the annuity that had grown from $20,000 to $55,000, only the $6,000 would be taxed. Subsequent redemptions would be taxed in the year of distribution; the final $20,000 would not be taxed since it represents principal. (You cannot claim that the first money withdrawn was contributed dollars and therefore not taxable. The IRS no longer allows this option for contracts purchased after 1981.)

Participants in annuities purchased before 1981 can opt to withdraw principal first and growth or interest later. By utilizing such a strategy, no taxes would be paid on any of the redemptions until such cumulative withdrawals equaled the contract owner's contributions (principal).

The avoidance of income taxes can continue indefinitely. The death of the annuitant would normally mean that the contract is terminated. However, if one spouse is named as the contract owner and annuitant and the other spouse is named as the beneficiary, the contract can continue. The surviving spouse has the option of liquidating part or all of the investment without cost, fee, or penalty by either the IRS or the issuer (the insurance company). Withdrawals or complete liquidations trigger an income tax event to the extent that any monies the survivor receives are considered growth or interest.

In this example, the surviving spouse does not have to terminate the contract upon the death of the other spouse. The remaining spouse can take over the investment and postpone any income tax event. The contract would then continue until the death of the surviving spouse. If the remaining spouse later remarries and names the new spouse as the beneficiary, the tax deferral could last until the death of both of these spouses.

Upon the death of the final spouse, the nonspousal beneficiaries are entitled to the proceeds. These beneficiaries have four choices: (1) Pay taxes immediately; (2) make withdrawals during the next five years and pay taxes along the way; (3) wait up to five years, make a complete liquidation, and then pay taxes; or (4) annuitize (a concept that will be discussed in a later chapter) and pay some taxes with each withdrawal. Each of these options is discussed next using the same example.

Let us suppose that Mary and John Smith bought an annuity in 1984 for $40,000. John dies in 1990 and Mary dies in 1992; the children inherit an annuity that is now worth $100,000. The beneficiaries could withdraw the entire $100,000 and pay income taxes on the $60,000 gain. A taxable event would occur in the calendar year in which the $60,000 was received.

The children, or whomever the beneficiaries are, do not have to take the proceeds from the annuity upon death of the final spouse; they have the option of making withdrawals systematically or sporadically during the next five years. Any amount withdrawn would be taxed in the year in which it was received. If the children took out $15,000 in 1993, then taxes would be due on $15,000 worth of "income" received for the 1993 calendar year. If $10,000 more was taken out in 1994, taxes would be due on that amount for the 1994 calendar year. If this option is used, the only IRS requirement is that the contract must be completely liquidated within five years after the death of the final spouse. In our example of $40,000 growing to $100,000, the final $40,000 withdrawn would not be taxed since it is still considered a return of principal.

The third option is to let the $100,000 contract continue to grow and compound tax deferred for up to five years, and then liquidate and pay taxes. At the end of five years, let us suppose that the contract is worth $165,000. The beneficiaries would be required to liquidate the entire investment and pay taxes on the difference between the amount withdrawn and principal ($165,000 − $40,000 = taxes due on $125,000 gain). The beneficiaries do not have to wait five years to make a complete liquidation. The entire amount can be withdrawn anytime during this five-year period.

The fourth option is *annuitization*. The beneficiary must choose annuitization within 12 months after the death of the surviving spouse. Annuitization simply means that the beneficiary will receive a specific amount each month until his or her share, plus any accumulating interest or growth, has been completely withdrawn. These withdrawals have a certain tax benefit because the IRS considers a portion of each check to be a return of principal and therefore not taxable.

Tax-Free Exchanges

Sometimes you go into one investment and later discover that it is not what you wanted or its quality has changed. One of the advantages of annuities is that you can change companies for whatever reason you like. You simply have your money moved from one annuity to another.

This move is known as a *1035 exchange* (after the Internal Revenue Code, or IRC, section that allows such exchanges) or a *tax-free exchange* since you do not pay any taxes. Always keep in mind that the only time you pay taxes on the growth or interest in an annuity is when you make withdrawals or a complete liquidation.

To take advantage of a tax-free exchange, the money from one insurer must go directly to another insurance company. You cannot have the check sent to you first. The IRS allows such 1035 exchanges because the money is never seen or touched by anyone except the insurers.

Tax-free exchanges are simple to do. You simply find a new annuity (company) you want to have the contract moved to and fill out the company's application along with a separate form identified as a 1035 exchange request. You then send these two forms along with your existing contract to the new company. The new insurer takes care of the rest. If you cannot find your existing contract, which is usually a few dozen pages in length, you simply fill out a lost contract form and send it to the company you want your assets transferred to.

You do not have to contact the person who sold you the original annuity. The lost contract form and 1035 exchange request are each less than a page in length. You can make a tax-free exchange at any time. You are not limited by number of exchanges per year.

Although 1035 exchanges are straightforward and do not trigger an IRS penalty or tax, the insurance company may charge a penalty. Whether or not an insurance company penalty will occur depends on the specifics of the contract. Normally, no penalties occur if the money has stayed with the original issuer for a certain number of years. With some companies this period is as little as one year. However, most insurers have a penalty schedule that lasts for five to seven years. A few policies have a penalty that never disappears.

The next chapter will explain the aforementioned penalties in detail as well as how to avoid such penalties.

Performance

Fixed-Rate Annuities

Fixed-rate accounts offer you a specific rate of return for a specified time; the rate is guaranteed for this period. The interest rate you are guaranteed varies depending on the annuity you choose. If you do a little homework, you can get a rate that is similar to or higher than a bank CD or money market account.

Variable Annuities

Since variable annuities offer several different subaccounts, ranging from conservative to aggressive, the selection process is more difficult. You can make the decision-making process much simpler by first deciding what you are trying to do with your money.

For instance, if you were looking for a variable annuity that offered a growth and income account as well as an international securities portfolio, you could limit your advisor's research to insurers that offered at least these two subaccounts. The advisor could then study these annuities for any performance or safety concerns that were important to you.

The important thing to remember about both fixed-rate and variable annuities is that they offer some tremendous benefits without sacrificing performance. Fixed-rate accounts offer similar or higher rates than other investments that have comparable safety. The subaccounts (growth, government securities, corporate bond, money market, etc.) within variable annuities can equal or exceed the performance of the highest-rated mutual funds.

Professional Management

One of the difficult parts about dealing with stockbrokers is that no one ranks their performance. But if you ask brokers how well they have done for their clients, they will all say "fantastic." There is no source or agency to dispute such claims. If all brokers have done a great job for their clients, who are all of those people who have lost money?

The truth is that millions of people have lost money with their stockbroker, financial planner, accountant, and so on. It is equally true that lots of people have lost money in most types of mutual funds and *variable* annuities. To a certain degree, losses and profits are due to management.

It is not that most brokers or investment advisors are bad; it is that they are at a great disadvantage. Stockbrokers, accountants, financial planners, and so on are busy trying to do several things: going to meetings, talking to clients, trying to get new accounts, learning about new investments, reading about tax law changes, or handling some administrative task.

The professional manager or investment team that is overseeing your annuity portfolio is a specialist. The portfolio managers do not talk to clients or do anything else that might interfere with the job they were hired to do: manage your money. These professionals are highly skilled and trained. They are specialists who focus on a certain segment of the marketplace. When you need heart surgery, you go to a heart specialist and not a general practitioner. Annuity management is structured the same way. The people running a government bond portfolio concentrate on obtaining the very best securities for their investors—people like you and me.

There are several independent sources that track the performance of fixed-rate and variable annuities. Some of these outside rating services are Morningstar, Lipper Analytical Services, VARDS, and Standard & Poor's. Magazines and periodicals, such as *The Wall Street Journal* and *Barron's*, also run articles periodically that discuss annuities and chart their performance.

No Commission Charges

Whether you invest in a fixed-rate or variable annuity, 100% of your money goes to work for you from day 1. You pay no commission when you go into an annuity. Furthermore, you do not pay a commission when you withdraw part of the account or liquidate the entire contract (after a certain time period).

Even though stockbrokers and financial planners are often "wearing too many hats," some of these professionals are well versed when it comes to annuity selections. The broker or advisor you deal with is paid a commission from the insurance company. So bypassing your stockbroker, insurance agent, or financial planner does not benefit you in the least. The insurance company will either keep the commission or pay it out to one of its producers (e.g., agents, brokers, planners, etc.).

Since the insurance company (annuity issuer) pays the commission, it is in your best interest to make sure that someone who can help you later receives the fee. If your agent or advisor receives the fee, he or she will feel obligated to answer any questions or facilitate any changes you might make now or in the future. This person can also research other companies if your annuity somehow becomes shaky or fails to perform as expected.

Annuities are referred to as *no load* or *commission free* since any commission paid comes directly from the insurance company's pocket. The commission normally ranges from 1 to 6 percent; the exact amount depends on the type of annuity and the penalty period. The most common rate that an annuity company pays is 4 percent.

Sending your money directly to the insurance company will not save you anything. A much better strategy is to make sure that your representative, whether he or she works at a bank, savings and loan, brokerage firm, insurance agency, or financial planning group, knows that you are going through him or her and that you expect quality service and advice in the future.

Withdrawal Options

You can take out part or all of your money at any time from a fixed-rate or variable annuity. However, the withdrawal may be subject to a penalty.

Most annuities allow withdrawals of up to 10% per year without cost, fee, or penalty. The free withdrawal is usually based on a percentage of your principal, not current value. Thus, if Cindy Boyd invests $50,000 in an annuity, she can withdraw $5,000 each year, *after the first year*, without any cost. This is true even though her account has a current value of $90,000. Some companies calculate the free withdrawal based on *the greater of* current value or principal contribution(s). In such a case, Cindy could withdraw $9,000 (10% of $90,000).

A few companies allow withdrawals of up to 15% per year. Whatever rate your company allows, keep in mind two points: (1) Close to 75% of all people who invest in an annuity never take any money out, and (2) the restrictions on withdrawals eventually disappear.

The aforementioned restrictions simply mean that you can take out more than, say, 10% per year, but you will pay a penalty. The amount of penalty depends on the type of contract you have and the insurance company you use. Some annuities let you take out all of your money at the end of every year without cost, fee, or penalty; withdrawals *during* the year may eat into part of the credited interest but cannot eat into your principal (unlike the penalties found in a CD). Other annuities impose a penalty for excess withdrawals during the first five, six, seven, or eight years. A small number of companies impose a penalty on "excess" withdrawals at any time during the life of the contract. Penalties are discussed in the next chapter, but an example may be helpful here.

Suppose that you invested $500,000 in the GHI annuity and the account is currently worth $800,000. As with most companies, GHI allows free annual withdrawals of up to 10%, based on the value of original contribution(s). In this case you could take out $50,000 each year without cost during the penalty period. At the end of five years, you could withdraw as much as you wanted from GHI without cost. But let us suppose during the first few years of the investment you needed $70,000. GHI would allow you to take out $50,000 during that year without cost. The remaining $20,000 you needed would be subject to a penalty. If this request was made during the second year of the investment, the penalty would probably be in the 5% range. The penalty is imposed only on the excess amount (the amount above the free withdrawal). In this example, 5%, or $1,000, would be charged (5% of $20,000). The investor would end up getting $69,000 of the $70,000 requested.

There are ways to avoid all penalties. These strategies are detailed in the next chapter.

Guaranteed Death Benefit

Your principal is guaranteed every day in a fixed-rate annuity. A guaranteed death benefit is of no added benefit for an investment that carries such an assurance. Thus, this section deals with *variable* annuities only.

When you invest in a variable annuity, it automatically contains a guaranteed death benefit. The guarantee works as follows: Upon the death of the annuitant, the beneficiary will receive the greater of the principal, plus any ongoing additions, or the value of the account as of the annuitant's date of death.

This guaranteed death benefit makes the variable annuity an ideal investment for an older couple that wants a high income stream or growth to offset inflation. One spouse can name himself or herself as the annuitant and invest in one or more of the stock or bond subaccounts, knowing that upon death the survivor will get back the greater of the amount invested or the current value of the annuity.

For example, suppose that Mr. and Mrs. Nathan Baty invest $400,000 in a variable annuity and Mr. Baty names himself as the annuitant. He feels lucky, and he decides to put the entire $400,000 into an aggressive stock portfolio. A few months or years later, there is a stock market crash, recession, depression, and/or other terrible events. The account drops in value to $5,000; the Batys have lost $395,000. But have they? Later, Mr. Baty is in an accident and dies. Mrs. Baty will receive $400,000 as the beneficiary, even though the account on Mr. Baty's death was worth approximately $5,000.

The guaranteed death benefit is based on the greater of all contributions (investments made by the owner) or value on the date of the annuitant's death, whichever is higher. Suppose in the preceding example that during the Batys' lifetimes the $400,000 grew to

$1,200,000, dropped to $50,000, went up to $900,000, and then dropped to $750,000 on the date of Mr. Baty's death. Mrs. Baty would be entitled to $750,000. She is not entitled to the peak value of the account during the annuitant's lifetime.

If the Batys originally invested $400,000 and then later added another $500,000, the minimum death benefit would be $900,000, reduced by any withdrawals made from the account. It would not be fair to the insurance company if it reimbursed you for money you had voluntarily taken out before the annuitant's death.

The guaranteed death benefit lasts until you terminate the contract, annuitize the investment, the annuitant dies, or the annuitant reaches a certain age (usually 75 or 80).

Avoidance of Probate

Probate is a messy, lengthy, and expensive process. It took over 15 years to probate the estate of Howard Hughes and over 10 years in the case of Marilyn Monroe. The lawyers who probated John Wayne's estate made so much money in the process that they closed down their firm once The Duke's estate was finally settled.

The amount you will spend on probate and executor (the person who settles your estate after you die) fees depends on the *gross* value of your estate (e.g., the value of all of your assets, clothes, boats, cars, stocks, bank accounts, and real estate, *not* reduced by any outstanding mortgages or debts). An estate that has a gross value of $100,000 will pay court-ordered fees of up to $6,300. Probate and executor fees increase as the size of your estate increases. These fees may be much higher than you think since (1) your estate will probably increase in value between now and the date of your death, and (2) the lawyer who probates the estate can always petition the court for additional or extraordinary fees.

Probate fees are not easily negotiable. They are based on a set schedule. The only fees that can usually be negotiated are those of the executor.

Fortunately, the value of your annuity will not be included when your gross estate is valued. All annuities avoid probate. The beneficiary receives the investment immediately without cost, fee, commission, or probate fees. Equally important, there is no delay. The beneficiary(s) can get their hands on the money within a few days after the annuitant's death.

Commonly Asked Questions

What does tax deferral mean to me?

It means you pay no taxes on the interest your annuity earns, as long
as that interest remains in the contract. The money that would
otherwise go to the government goes to work for you instead—
compounding and building even more tax-deferred interest. The
cumulative effect of this tax deferral can be startling. Your funds
grow much faster, as shown in Figure 3.1.

The rate of return indicated in Figure 3.1 is hypothetical and is
not intended to indicate the actual performance of any particular
fixed annuity. Income taxes are payable upon withdrawal or distribution, and a 10% penalty tax may apply to withdrawals made before
age 59.5.

How does an annuity compare to an IRA for retirement?

Annuities and IRAs differ in a number of significant areas. Not
everyone can open an IRA—only those with earned income. Any-

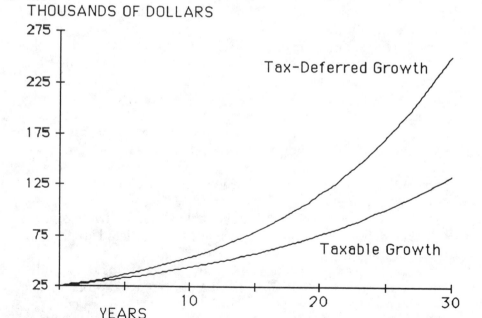

FIGURE 3.1 **A Tax-Deferred Versus a Taxable Investment of
$25,000 at 8% Return (Assuming 28% Marginal Tax Bracket).**

one can purchase a fixed-rate or variable annuity. When it is time to contribute, you will be limited to $2,000 annually with an IRA; there are no limits (except for a possible minimum) with an annuity.

IRA contributions may be tax deductible, although the law now imposes limits based on income and pension-plan coverage. Generally, no deductions are allowed for payments to an annuity. If you are not allowed a deduction for your IRA contribution, an annuity is a smart alternative—your money still grows tax deferred. If you are eligible to make tax-deductible payments to an IRA, consider an individual retirement annuity, which allows you to enjoy the advantages of both the IRA and the annuity.

When it comes time to begin withdrawals, annuities generally provide one unique and important advantage: If you annuitize, you can receive an income for life, even if you ultimately receive more than the total value of your account. With most IRAs, you have no such guarantee.

How important is professional management?

When you invest in an annuity, you have hired professional management. Individually, you and I cannot afford to hire the same money managers as the Kennedys and Rockefellers, but *collectively* we can hire even better performers. By hiring professionals to manage your money, you do not have to worry about the day-to-day fluctuations in the stock and bond market or wonder if the securities purchased are about to be downgraded. A money management team takes care of all of this. You and I are free to concentrate on other things: raising a family, getting a larger salary, taking up a hobby, and so on.

Are tax-free exchanges easier than shifting traditional investments?

You may think that you will never want to move your money from a mutual fund, stock, bond, or bank CD, but think again. No one knows where interest rates will be in a couple of years or if a bank may become troubled or when a money manager leaves a certain mutual fund. When such an event occurs, you may be reluctant to move your money either due to a sense of safety (comfort level in dealing with the same institution year after year) or because of the tax ramifications. With annuities you can easily move your money from one well-known company to another without triggering a tax event. Simply by filling out a form, money is conveniently and quickly moved from one insurer to another.

How important are rates within an annuity?

Even a fraction of a percent is important in calculating returns for the life of an annuity. Everything adds up, and rate (or yield or total return) shopping is a critical factor in choosing an annuity. The insurance company itself is of secondary importance to the performance of the subaccounts within an annuity.

CHAPTER 4

The Disadvantages of Annuity Investing

The previous chapter focused on the many advantages of both fixed-rate and variable annuities. You probably are thinking that annuities seem like the perfect investment. But before you rush out and invest all of your money in an annuity, read this chapter to learn about the negative points of annuity investing. Fortunately, the disadvantages of annuities are few; most of them will not apply to you.

The disadvantages of annuities are (1) potential IRS penalties and taxes (for individuals under the age of 59.5), (2) potential insurance company penalties, and (3) the ongoing expenses of variable annuities.

IRS Penalties

No matter what type of annuity you purchase, it is subject to a 10% IRS penalty for withdrawals of growth or income made prior to age 59.5. No penalty is imposed on your principal contributions when they are taken out. There are four ways to avoid the 10% penalty: (1) death of the annuitant, (2) disability of the annuitant, (3) annuitization, or (4) the contract owner reaching age 59.5 or older.

It does not matter how old the annuitant is. If he or she dies, all IRS penalties are waived. Disability is defined in Section 72 of the Internal Revenue Code. The death or disability of the annuitant, *not* the contract owner or beneficiary, will prevent an IRS penalty.

Annuitization (in which a portion of the annuity's assets are paid out as income on a regular basis) will also prevent any penalty, but the contract owner must elect annuitization within one year after investing in the annuity. The final way in which the 10% IRS penalty can be avoided is obvious: reaching age 59.5 or older. The measuring life here is the contract owner, not the annuitant.

Because of the potential IRS penalty, annuities are not recommended for younger people unless the investment is part of a retirement plan, such as an IRA, Keogh, pension, or profit-sharing plan, or unless the contract owner is an individual or couple who will not need to touch the funds except in an emergency. Therefore, fixed-rate and variable annuities are ideal candidates for the investor who is near or past age 59.5.

The contract owner(s) can be any age, ranging from newborn to over 110. Annuities do make sense for a young individual or couple, depending on how soon the money is withdrawn from the account and the assumed rate of growth. That is, the pre-59.5 penalty can be more than offset by the compounding of whole (pre-tax) dollars if the rate of return is in the 14% range and no withdrawals are made for at least six years.

For example, suppose that Susan Trump, age 25, invests $10,000 in a variable annuity that ends up giving her an average annual compound rate of return of 15%. At this rate of return, her $10,000 will more than double and be worth $20,113 in five years. Further suppose that at the end of five years, due to an emergency, she wants to withdraw her $20,113, and death or disability of the annuitant has not occurred. Before she received her $20,113, she would have to pay a 10% penalty on the growth portion of her annuity ($10,113 in this example). A 10% penalty on $10,113 equals $1,011. Susan would receive $19,102 and would be subject to income taxes on the $10,113 worth of growth and/or income.

The income tax liability is not reduced by the amount of the penalty, so Susan would be subject to ordinary income tax on the $10,113 gross growth figure, not the $9,102 after-penalty amount.

Based on Susan's state and federal tax bracket combined (a hypothetical 33% for our example), she would pay $3,337 in state and federal income taxes. Her net proceeds would be $15,765 based on the following calculation: $10,113 minus $1,011 in penalties minus $3,337 in taxes plus her original investment of $10,000, which is not subject to taxes or penalties.

As bad as Susan's situation might seem, contrast it to someone who also invested $10,000 and received the same 15% annual compound rate of return. But let's say this investor did not go into an annuity and was taxed on the full 15% gain each year. Assuming the same 33% combined tax bracket, this investor would end up with $16,105, a figure only slightly higher than Susan Trump's figure.

If you take into account the aforementioned facts, but assume that Susan did not cancel her annuity contract for 10 years, the picture changes. At the end of 10 years, Susan's $10,000 is now worth slightly more than $40,000. After paying the 10% IRS penalty of $3,000 (10% of $30,000) and $10,000 in ordinary income tax (33% of $30,000), Susan will net $27,000. Her counterpart, who was not in an annuity and ended up paying taxes on the 15% gain each year, ended up with $26,620 at the end of the same 10 years.

We can see from the previous example that if a younger couple or individual can live with a variable annuity for approximately five years, the results are only slightly lower than paying taxes on an ongoing basis in an alternative investment. At the end of 10 years, the annuity owner is often better off than the nonsheltered investor.

The preceding example assumes a worst-case situation: an annuity contract that is subject to a 10% IRS penalty. Remember that this penalty does not apply to any contract owner (investor) who is age 59.5 or older and that the penalty can also be waived by death or disability of the owner or death of the annuitant.

Income Taxes

An investment in an annuity means that your money will grow and compound tax deferred, not tax free. Any and all income tax liability can be postponed indefinitely. The previous chapter noted that the death of one spouse would not trigger income taxes if the beneficiary was the surviving spouse. Taxes can be further deferred if the surviving spouse remarries, naming himself or herself as the annuitant and the new partner as the beneficiary. When both spouses die, the beneficiaries (i.e., children, nephews, friends, etc.) can postpone taxes for up to an additional five years.

At some time, income taxes will have to be paid. There is no "step up in basis" or other technique to avoid taxes forever. The tax liability is the difference between the amount(s) invested subtracted from the value of the annuity contract, multiplied by the beneficiary's tax bracket. As an example, suppose Ursel Jones invested $10,000 in an annuity several years ago. Two years ago, she added another $5,000. Last month, Ursel died, and the annuity was inherited by her friend,

Sven Haynie. Mr. Haynie waits five more years (the maximum time limit for a nonspouse) and liquidates the entire contract, which is now worth $40,000. His tax liability is calculated as follows: $40,000 − ($10,000 + $5,000) × 28% (his federal tax bracket). In other words, he will owe $7,000 in federal income taxes. A similar computation would also be made for state income taxes.

Fortunately, the eventuality of paying taxes is not all bad. Since you are the owner of the annuity, you decide when withdrawals are to be made. Hopefully, you will take out money only when you are in a low or lower tax bracket—obviously, it is much better to pay income taxes at a 15% rate rather than a 28% rate. To illustrate the advantage of tax-deferred growth which is eventually taxed versus an investment that grows at the same rate but is taxed each year, let us look at an example.

Suppose you and your neighbor each have $1,000,000 to invest and you are both in a 33% tax bracket, state and federal combined. You both have decided on an investment that should average 15% per year. Your neighbor invests the entire $1,000,000 in a growth and income mutual fund; you invest your $1,000,000 in a growth and income portfolio within a variable annuity. Assuming a 20-year time horizon and a 15% pretax rate of return, the final numbers are impressive for the variable annuity owner.

At the end of 20 years, you have amassed over $16,000,000. After paying income taxes of $5,000,000, you net a little over $11,000,000. Your neighbor, who was paying income taxes every year for 20 years, ends up netting approximately $6,829,000. You do not have to be a rocket scientist to see the advantage that the annuity offers—over $4,000,000.

The case for the annuity owner becomes even stronger if some of the withdrawals were made while in a lower tax bracket. This would be a strong possibility since the owner decides when liquidations are made.

The annuity investor looks even stronger if we assume that the investor is a set of older owners who are receiving social security benefits. Up to one half of an individual's social security benefits can be taxed. This social security tax kicks in if you are single and have an adjusted gross income of $25,000 or more ($32,000 or more if you are married and file a joint return). The formula used to determine the $25,000 and $32,000 levels includes all sources of income, including interest from tax-free bonds *and* social security payments. The formula does *not* include the deferred growth or income within an annuity.

Insurance Company Penalties

Whether or not the IRS penalty is applicable to you, you must be aware of any potential annuity penalty. This penalty, often called a *surrender charge*, only applies if you take out a certain amount of money from your contract within a set number of years.

When you invest in an annuity, you can make noncumulative annual withdrawals of 10% per year without penalty, after the first year. (At least one company allows withdrawals of up to 15% per year without penalty.) An insurance company penalty occurs if you take out an amount in excess of that free withdrawal privilege. For example, if you invested $90,000 in an annuity, you could withdraw $9,000 per year without penalty. At the end of a set number of years, you could withdraw any amount without penalty. However, let us suppose that during one of the first few years of the contract you needed $15,000. The amount in excess of the free withdrawal, $6,000 ($15,000 needed minus the $9,000 allowed), would be subject to a penalty. The amount of the penalty varies depending on the insurance company's penalty schedule, but it would probably amount to approximately 4% in this example. Based on a 4% penalty, $240 would be subtracted from your withdrawal request. The initial $15,000 request would result in a net amount of $14,760 to you.

When shopping for an annuity, you or your advisor should look at the insurance company's penalty schedule. The penalty period could last for 10 or more years, and the penalty itself could be as high as 10% for the entire 10-year period. Fortunately, most companies have a penalty period that lasts for only five to seven years. The penalty itself usually declines each year.

For example, the LMN annuity may state that its penalty lasts for six years and is structured as "6-5-4-3-2-1-0 thereafter." This means that a withdrawal made during the first year would be subject to a 6% penalty; money taken out during the second year would be penalized 5%, and so on.

There are ways to avoid this penalty schedule: (1) death of the annuitant, (2) disability of the annuitant (with most companies), (3) annuitization, (4) limiting withdrawals to those allowed under the free withdrawal privilege, (5) waiting until the penalty period lapses, and (6) adopting a systematic withdrawal plan of up to 10% per year.

As inhibiting as the penalty may appear to you, it is important to note that if an emergency arises you will probably have other sources of capital to tap into. Even if you needed to take money out of your annuity, it would be even more doubtful that it would exceed the free percentage withdrawal.

Mortality and Expense Fee

The mortality and expense fee, also known as the *guaranteed death benefit*, is a feature of all variable annuities; fixed-rate contracts do not possess this charge. This fee is levied against your account balance every year. It is the insurance industry's major, and perhaps by some measurements only, source of profit. This fee helps to cover the insurer's overhead, reimburse it for the commission paid out to the agent who sold you the contract, pay for the set-up and issuance of the annuity policy, and act as a "war chest" to pay off any death benefit claims.

The death benefit charge ranges from 1.1% to 1.5% annually, depending on the insurer and the terms of the variable annuity contract. The most common mortality charge is 1.2%. Whatever the fee that your particular insurer charges, it can never be increased; every variable annuity contract specifies clearly that the fee is "frozen." The fee is hidden in that it is not shown on any of your quarterly or annual statements. It is described in the prospectus.

You must be given a prospectus at, or prior to, the time of purchasing a variable annuity. The prospectus spells out the different types of subaccounts within the variable annuity, charts the previous performance of these investments, and lists any and all charges that will be deducted from your variable annuity portfolio(s).

The mortality fee is a small percentage figure based on the total value of your variable annuity. The greater your account grows, the more the insurance company will end up collecting. Thus, if the annual mortality charge is 1.3%, a $10,000 account will be charged $130 per year. When the investment grows to $15,000, the yearly charge will increase to $195.

There are three good things that you can say about the mortality charge. First, it helps to pay for commission and overhead costs that you would normally pay in the form of an up-front or ongoing sales charge. Second, it gives the insurance company an incentive to hire the best possible money managers for each portfolio. Since the insurer makes more money if your account grows, it wants to make sure you do well. Conversely, if the account shrinks in value, you both lose. Third, the mortality charge insures the integrity of the guaranteed death benefit.

As you may recall from the previous chapter, the guaranteed death benefit provides that, upon the annuitant's death, the beneficiary will receive *the greater of* the original investment(s) or account value at death.

For example, Cindy Boyd and Clint Westwood decide to invest $250,000 in a variable annuity. A few months later, they add another $50,000; three years later they add $100,000 more. Their contributions total $400,000.

While both Cindy and Clint are alive, they make a few withdrawals due to unforeseen circumstances. The partial liquidations which take place over several years total $80,000. A few months after they have made the last withdrawal, Clint, who was named as the annuitant, dies. At the date of his death, the annuity is worth only $130,000 due to some very poor investment results. However, because of the guaranteed death benefit, Cindy, who was named as the beneficiary, will receive $320,000 ($400,000 contributed minus the $80,000 withdrawn). If the account at Clint's death was worth $900,000, Cindy would receive $900,000.

You cannot find this type of guaranteed benefit with any other type of investment. It provides an individual or couple with peace of mind. Remember that this charge only applies to variable annuities; principal is always guaranteed in a fixed-rate annuity.

Annual Contract Maintenance Charge

The contract maintenance charge is minor compared to the mortality fee. The annual contract maintenance charge ranges from $25 to $50, depending on the variable annuity company. The most common charge is $35 per year.

The maintenance charge shows up on your fourth-quarter statement issued by the insurer. It is deducted from the then-current value of your variable annuity. The fee is the same for a $5,000 investment or a $1,000,000 contract; it is a flat charge.

The only good thing that can be said about this fee is that it can never increase. The wording in every variable annuity states that the annual contract maintenance fee cannot be increased during the life of the contract.

You could compare this maintenance fee to the typical $5 fee charged by a mutual fund family whenever switches within the family occur (e.g., you decide to move part of your money from the XYZ stock fund to the XYZ bond fund). Every time you move money within a mutual fund family, your account is charged $5. In the case of variable annuities, there is no charge for making such moves among the various portfolios.

Commonly Asked Questions

If I'm 59.5 or older, what's the difference if I take a lump sum distribution or annuitize?

Taking the lump sum would subject the entire growth and/or accumulated interest in the contract to income taxes (if it wasn't rolled over into some type of tax-advantaged investment). Annuitization only subjects a portion of the amount withdrawn for that year to tax.

What if I withdraw my entire annuity investment but later decide to put the entire amount back in? Will I be subject to a tax or insurance company penalty?

If you let your insurance company know your intentions, there is usually a grace period for withdrawals. But the IRS is not forgiving. Monies cannot flow in and out of annuities (subject to IRS and insurance company rules) without a tax imposed.

What will the insurance company charge for its services?

Charges vary from company to company, but the most common charge is called a surrender charge and comes into play only if you decide to withdraw all or part of your money before a certain number of years (specified in the contract) have passed.

Will I have access to my money if I need it?

Annuity contracts generally provide several liquidity features. Depending on your specific contract and how long it has been in force, you may be able to withdraw a certain dollar amount or a portion of your contract without charge. In other cases, you may incur a surrender charge. If you withdraw all your money, you surrender the contract and it terminates. The surrender benefit is generally equal to your contract value (premiums plus interest and any growth) minus any surrender charges.

Are annuities safer than other investments?

Consider the following occurrences: In the 1980s, California residents did not think that they could ever lose money in real estate. By the early 1990s, some of these same land owners were unable to unload their properties at any price. Between 1982 and 1987, it looked as if stocks were going to increase in value forever; then came the October 19, 1987 stock market crash, when most investors experienced over a 20% loss in one day. Certificate of deposit investors were thrilled when CD rates were in the high teens in the early 1980s. By the early 1990s, CD yields were less than 4%. And who would have thought that the price of oil could go from $35 to $10 per barrel in less than a decade?

CHAPTER 5

The Intricacies of Fixed-Rate Annuities

This chapter discusses all the features of a fixed-rate account. Chapter 6 details the different aspects of variable annuities. It is much lengthier than this chapter since variable accounts are more complex than their fixed counterparts.

All fixed-rate annuities possess the following features: (1) a guaranteed amount at the end of a specific period, (2) free bail-out provision, (3) the ability to add new contracts, (4) a secured future program, and (5) tax-favored annuitization.

The Guarantees

As you know, principal in a fixed annuity is guaranteed every day. You can also be assured that at the end of a specified time period, you have an amount you can count on.

When you invest in a fixed-rate annuity, you decide on a rate of return to lock in. Typically, the longer you are willing to commit, the higher the rate you will get (sort of like investing in a bank CD). The annuity contract you are looking at may provide the following choices: one year at 7.5%, three years at 7.75%, or five years at 8.10%. You must choose one of the options. Whatever option you choose, the rate of return is guaranteed to be what is stated. Thus, if you wanted the three-year option at 7.75%, you would get 7.75% compounded annually for exactly three years whether or not interest rates went up, the stock market declined, or the economy went into a recession during that time.

The aforementioned rates are for illustration purposes. The different rate options and periods of time for which such rates are locked in depend on the company you are looking at and the general level of interest rates. You will usually find that the range of rates offered are somewhat higher than those rates offered by CDs or money market accounts.

The example given in Figure 5.1 shows the tax advantage of a fixed-rate annuity versus a certificate of deposit. The example assumes a $100,000 original investment, a taxpayer who is in the 28% bracket, and that both types of investments are earning 9% annually. As you can see from this example, the annuity investor comes out ahead *every year*.

The question often arises regarding how long you should tie up your money. The answer depends on what you think will happen to interest rates in the future. If you think that interest rates will go up during the next several years, choose a one-year contract. At the end of the year, you can roll over your annuity into a higher rate, either with the same or a different company. If you think rates will be falling, choose the longest term offered, usually 5 to 10 years. If

Year	Certificate of Deposit		Fixed Annuity
1	$106,480.00		$109,000.00
2	$111,565.50		$118,810.00
3	$115,556.60		$129,502.90
4	$118,688.82		$141,158.16
5	$121,146.99		$153,862.39
		Total	$153,862.39
		Less tax	− 15,081.47
Total	$121,146.99	Total	$138,780.92
	Difference:	$17,633.93	Annuity advantage

FIGURE 5.1 **Illustration of Tax Advantage.**

interest rates do fall, you will be thankful that you are getting a yield on your investment that none of your friends can touch.

If you are uncertain about the direction of interest rates, opt for something in the middle: a two-, three-, or four-year guarantee period. This middle-of-the-road approach means that you are not committed for any unbearable period of time. If rates fall, you will still be getting a higher rate for at least a few years. If rates go up, your lower rate of return can be moved into a higher rate in a couple of years.

In addition to the aforementioned guaranteed rates and periods, fixed-rate annuities provide an absolute minimum guarantee, exclusive of other interest rates or the state of the economy. This rate ranges from 4% to 6% but is almost always 4%. Thus, if bank CDs, the prime interest rate, or other generally followed interest rates fall to 2% or 3%, you are guaranteed at least 4% in a fixed-rate annuity.

In the world of investments, we often lose sight of history. A few decades ago, many traditional investments had returns of well under 3%. And, although it is hard to imagine such a situation in the foreseeable future, think back to the 1980s. In 1981, the prime interest rate peaked briefly at 21.5%. When it hit this rate, many investment advisors and financial gurus felt that the prime would not stop until it hit 25% or 30%. Few, if any, predicted that the prime would actually fall by over two thirds. Yet, during the final year of the Reagan presidency, the prime rate dropped to 7.75%. By the end of Bush's first term, the prime lending rate was in the 6% range. So you can see that what we may currently think of as amazing can turn out to be humdrum and ordinary.

The length of time you choose is your decision; however, you cannot alter the rate specified by the insurer. If at any time you are not satisfied with the contract, you can cancel it and invest in another annuity. Whether or not your former company will levy a penalty against your investment depends on the specific provisions of the contract. Even if your former company hits you with a penalty, there is a chance that the new insurer will absorb part or all of it.

Free Bail-Out

The free bail-out provision is closely tied to the guaranteed interest rate provision of a fixed-rate annuity. It can prove to be highly beneficial to the contract owner.

The bail-out provision is straightforward: After the guaranteed interest rate period is over, if the renewal rate is ever less than 1% of the previously offered rate, the investor (contract owner) can liquidate part or all of the annuity, principal *and* interest, without cost, fee, or penalty. This provision gives the investor the security of knowing that he or she will always be getting a competitive rate.

For example, let us assume that you went into a fixed-rate annuity and decided on a three-year guaranteed rate of 8%. At the end of the three-year period, the insurer offers you a new rate of 6.99% for the next three years. You decide that there are other annuities or alternative investments that are more appealing. As long as you contact the insurance company within 30 days after receiving notice of the renewal rate, the annuity will be terminated and all of your principal, plus 8% compounded annually for three years, will be sent to you or whomever you direct the company to send the check to. You get this free bail-out since the renewal rate being offered was more than 1% lower than your previous locked-in rate.

Let us slightly change the facts in the preceding example. Suppose now that at the end of the first three years your annuity company offers you a renewal rate of 7% or higher. You have the choice of accepting the new rate, whether it is higher or lower than the past yield. But again, let us assume that you decide you need the money or have found a better place to invest. You can still withdraw all of the money, principal and interest, but you *may* be subject to an insurance company back-end penalty (described in Chapter 4).

Adding to Your Investment Holdings

An investment in a fixed-rate annuity is a contractual relationship. The insurance company guarantees you a rate of return based on a specific investment, no more and no less. With most companies, if you want to add more money, you must purchase another annuity.

For example, Peter Ward recently purchased a fixed-rate annuity with a locked-in rate of 8% for five years. A few weeks later, he decides to invest another $10,000 and would like to add to his existing annuity. Only a few insurers allow this. Pete will probably have to purchase another annuity at the then-current rates and terms. It may turn out that his best deal is with the insurer that he originally invested with. Nevertheless, even if he deals with this company, it will likely be a new and separate contract. The terms may end up being identical, but it must be a separate investment.

A Secured Future

One of the great features of a fixed-rate annuity is that you always know where you stand. There is an exact amount of money you can count on at the end of each period. A contract owner with $10,000 who signs up for a five-year annuity that guarantees an 8% return knows that there will be exactly $14,693 in the account at the end of the five years ($10,000 × 1.08 × 1.08 × 1.08 × 1.08 × 1.08 = $14,693).

The annuity contract will tell you what you can expect in the way of growth of principal, and it will detail the exact amount of any penalties or fees that may exist and when such costs disappear.

Annuitization: Tax-Favored Checks

Annuitization is a process that the contract owner elects. It provides for the even distribution of both principal and interest over a period of time. The amount of each monthly, quarterly, or annual check will depend on the competitiveness of the insurer, the level of current interest rates, the amount of principal that is to be annuitized, and the duration of the withdrawals. Each of these points is discussed next.

Competition

When you shop for a money market or savings account, the rate that institutions offer will vary. Some companies are more competitive than others. The same is true in the case of annuitization. Some insurance companies may offer very attractive yields during the accumulation (growth) period but poor returns during disbursement (annuitization).

Current Interest Rates

The amount of each check you receive upon annuitization of a fixed-rate contract will be level; it will not go up or down with interest rates, the stock market, or the economy. The figure will be quoted on a per-$1,000 basis. For example, if you have a $13,000 contract, the insurer may quote you something like "$8 per thousand per month for the remainder of your life." This means that if you choose this company, you will be getting a check every month for exactly $104 ($8 times 13), or $1,248 annually for as many years as you live. If you live for 80 more years, the insurance company must send you those $104 monthly checks for the next 80 years.

If and when you decide to annuitize part or all of your investment, the amount you will receive monthly, quarterly, or annually will depend on current interest rates. If the insurer can take your money and invest it in a conservative manner such that it results in a high return to the company, a large portion of this would be passed on to you.

The previous paragraph may make it sound as if your ongoing return is based on what happens to the invested funds later on; this is not true. The amount of your check will stay level, no matter how lucky or unsuccessful the insurer is with its own portfolio. Nevertheless, current medium- and long-term interest rates greatly influence the rate the annuity company is willing to commit to at the time of your annuitization.

Principal to Be Distributed

Obviously, the larger the amount of capital that is to be returned to you, plus accumulating interest on the still-to-be-dispersed amounts, the greater each check will be.

Period of Annuitization

Someone who wants to annuitize $40,000 over a five-year period will get greater monthly checks than someone who wants to annuitize the same amount over a 10-year horizon. What makes the duration a little tricky is that annuitization does not have to be for a specific number of years.

When applying for an *immediate* annuity, an annuity payment mode is selected: monthly, quarterly, semiannually, or annually. The first annuity payment must be made no later than the end of the modal period selected. For example, if a contract is issued with a monthly mode on September 15, the first payment must be made on or before October 15.

Many people annuitize over a 3-, 5-, 10-year or longer period of time. Other contract owners want an income stream that will continue for the remainder of their life. Still others want monthly checks to continue during the lifetime of two people, such as a married couple, father and daughter, or two friends. Finally, a few people want the checks to last for a lifetime, theirs or someone else's, with a minimum guarantee of at least, say, 10 years. Each of these options is discussed next.

Life Annuity You can annuitize over a specific number of years. The only requirement is that the period of time be for at least three years. However, some investors want an income stream that they cannot outlive.

Under the lifetime option, checks continue to be received until the death of the annuitant. At the time of annuitization, you may decide to list the annuitant as yourself, your spouse, child, friend, or neighbor. The only requirement is that the person you choose is currently living and that the named annuitant signs the annuitization agreement.

All of the lifetime options share a common characteristic: The insurer is hoping that one or both annuitants die soon, and the investor hopes that the annuitant(s) lives for another 100 years. At the death of the annuitant(s), the balance of an account automatically goes to the *insurance company*, not to the heirs.

If you want your beneficiary(s) to get the balance of the account, you should either list them as a "co-annuitant" or opt for a period certain (i.e., complete disbursement of principal and interest over a specified period of time). By choosing a period certain, the insurance company may not benefit from a premature death.

Joint and Last Survivor Annuity The joint and last survivor option is usually chosen by a married couple or someone who provides support for another. Under this plan, checks are not stalled or altered after the death of the first person. The same amount continues to be sent out until the death of the survivor, whether that survivor is a spouse, son, daughter, friend, etc.

Under this option, one could say that the insurance company is hoping for the speedy death of two people (the death of one of the parties named does not do the company any good). The last survivor option is ideal for husbands or wives who want to make sure that their spouses continues to receive regular income after their death.

Lifetime with Period Certain Annuity A few people who choose one of the lifetime annuitization options want a certain minimum guarantee. Under this final alternative, checks continue until the annuitant dies. If death occurs before a period certain, checks continue until the period ends.

For example, if you chose your lifetime with a 10-year period certain and you died during the next 10 years, checks would continue to be sent to your beneficiary(s) for the remainder of the 10 years. The period certain does not begin when the annuitant dies; it is measured from the date of the original annuitization. Thus, if you died after having received monthly checks for seven years, your beneficiary would receive the same monthly checks for three more years.

If you favor a lifetime option, keep in mind that each option will not provide the same monthly check. Annuity issuers set their rates (amount they will pay you per $1,000 invested) based largely on life expectancy tables. If you are age 70, you will receive much more money each month than a 40-year-old who wishes to annuitize the same amount. The 40-year-old, who has a much longer life expectancy, will almost certainly receive a *cumulative* sum far greater than the 70-year-old.

A quick summary may be in order. Under all of the life options, the balance of the account, no matter how small or large, eventually reverts to the insurer. If a set number of years are chosen, such as annuitization over 3, 5, 10, or 20 years, all capital (principal) plus accumulated interest is dispersed, whether the annuitant is alive or deceased.

Tax-Advantaged Disbursements

The advantage of annuitization is that disbursements are tax favored; systematic and/or sporadic withdrawals are not. The disadvantage of annuitization is that the process, once started, cannot be altered and the rate of return during annuitization may be artificially low. Each of these points is discussed next.

The Exclusion Ratio   Upon annuitization, an exclusion ratio is automatically determined. The IRS uses this ratio, or formula, in determining the amount of each check received that is considered a return of capital and therefore not taxed. The amount considered growth and/or interest is fully taxed. An illustration may simplify this concept.

Assume that you have $100,000 to invest and you decide on a fixed-rate annuity. Further assume that you need as much current income as possible for the next five years. You therefore decide to annuitize your contract and request monthly checks. During the next 60 months (five years), approximately 85% of each check you receive will be considered a return of capital and therefore not taxed. The remaining 15% is considered income and taxed. Once all of the excluded amounts total $100,000, all remaining checks are considered to be 100% income and therefore taxed as ordinary income.

If, in the preceding example, you were sent monthly checks of $2,100, you would be taxed on only 15% of this amount until you received your fifty-seventh check (85%—the exclusion ratio in *this* example—of $2,100 equals $1,785; $100,000 divided by $1,785 equals 56. At the end of the fifty-sixth check, all $100,000 of principal will have been returned. All remaining checks are considered "gravy" and therefore are completely taxed).

The exclusion ratio varies depending on the life expectancy of the annuitant, based on mortality tables, or the set number of years the contract owner opted for. The longer the expected period, the smaller the exclusion ratio becomes.

Annuitization and Tax-Free Income

Combining an annuity program with what is called *seven-pay life insurance* can be a powerful move. The IRS allows you to borrow money *tax free* from the cash value in a life insurance policy if certain conditions are met—the "seven-pay test." Basically, the owner of the insurance policy needs to make sure that insurance premiums are paid in over a minimum period of time (a period that can be as little as five years).

As long as the seven-pay test is met, the only other thing the contract owner of the insurance policy must be aware of is that the vehicle maintain its "integrity" as a life insurance contract. This means that a contract owner cannot *cancel* the policy or borrow all of its cash value. If both of these tests are met, money can be borrowed freely from the insurance company every year, indefinitely.

Annuitization can work well in conjunction with seven-pay universal or whole life policies. A seven-year "period certain" immediate annuity funding a universal life contract is a good option for anyone who has a lump sum ready to deposit, wants to take advantage of the seven-pay life insurance test for future tax-free liquidity, and may also need a substantial death benefit. The advantages of this combination include that the client makes only one payment, the exclusion ratio on the immediate annuity makes the distributions about 80% tax free, and if the insured dies within the first six years the beneficiary of the annuitant receives the remaining payments.

By first making a lump-sum deposit into an annuity and requesting immediate annuitization over at least a five-year period, the investor is assured that the life insurance policy is funded properly. Immediate annuitization means that premiums are being paid when they should be, directly to the insurance company. This takes care of the seven-pay test and means that monies can be borrowed from the life insurance policy tax free as opposed to tax deferred.

Annuitization certainly offers some great tax benefits, but these benefits are not all considered tax free. By using a combination of an annuity that is annuitized and having the payments earmarked to pay for life insurance premiums, the investor can later take advantage of income that is 100% free of income taxes and receive some life insurance as a bonus.

People who seek this type of tax-free income will still have the opportunity to add more money to the life insurance policy after seven policy years. With *universal life*, the client can add some attractive riders to the policy, such as long-term health care, catastrophic illness, prime term, child or additional insured, and premium continuation for disability.

It is also possible to fund a final divorce or other legal action with an immediate annuity. With a cash refund annuity option, the cost would be only slightly more than a life-only annuity option. A cash refund option means that any undispersed monies will go to the beneficiary if the annuitant dies prior to a complete liquidation.

The CD/Annuity

During the past few years, a new type of fixed-rate annuity has emerged. It was created to satisfy the comfort level of people who were attracted to CDs. It also fulfills the needs of short-term investors. This relatively new type of fixed-rate annuity is known as a *CD/annuity*. It is given this name largely for marketing purposes.

The CD/annuity is a contract that has a one-year life. At the end of a year, the investor is free to take all of his or her money out, principal and interest, without any insurance company penalty, cost, or fee. The partial or complete liquidation can be sent directly to the contract owner or to another insurer. By using a 1035 tax-free exchange, the investor will not trigger a tax event. ("1035" refers to the Internal Revenue Code section that allows transfers between certain insurance products without being taxed.)

As you may recall from Chapter 3, if the proceeds are invested or deposited in a vehicle other than an annuity, a tax event will be triggered on the amount considered interest. A 10% IRS penalty will also occur if the contract owner is not at least 59.5 years old or the annuitant is not dead or disabled. The potential 10% penalty is also avoided under the provisions of the 1035 exchange.

As with any other type of investment, you should have your advisor seek out a CD/annuity that is offered by a secure insurer and offers the highest rate possible. If at the end of one year the existing insurer offers a rate that is acceptable to you, simply do nothing—your account will automatically be renewed, just like a CD maturing at a bank. If you do not like the renewal rate, for whatever reason, simply write to the annuity company within 30 days of receiving the renewal notice and instruct the company as to where you want the proceeds sent.

Summary

This chapter has covered the different features that fixed-rate annuities offer. The next chapter discusses the various aspects of variable annuity investing and points out why you may wish to consider using a variable annuity despite its uncertainties.

Commonly Asked Questions

What does the insurance company do with my fixed-rate premium?

The company invests the funds in its investment portfolio and credits interest to your account. This is called the *accumulation phase* of the contract. It is important during this phase to know that your annuity company manages its investments wisely. You want to choose a company that is highly rated by independent analysts for its ability to meet its obligations. The company should have a strong capital base and a history of quality service.

When will my annuity payments begin if my annuity is part of a qualified plan?

If your annuity is part of a qualified plan (IRA, Keogh, pension plan, etc.), the Internal Revenue Code generally requires that you begin taking payments by age 70.5. If the annuity is nonqualified, you will generally be required to begin receiving payments by age 85. Some companies never force you to take out any money, no matter how old you get. A number of insurers may offer immediate annuities, for which payments begin immediately.

What happens if I die before receiving any payments?

If you die before annuity payments begin, your beneficiary will receive a death benefit, usually equal to your total annuity value (premiums paid plus interest earned). This benefit avoids the costs and delays of probate.

How many annuities should I compare before I make a purchase?

As many as you can. The list of annuities and insurers in Appendix A is a good start. Also, your financial advisor should be able to point you in the right direction.

How can an insurance company guarantee me funds past the expected life of the annuity payment?

That is part of the deal. Insurance companies usually have good actuarial tables to project payouts. In the odd instance that an owner outlives his or her projections, insurance companies have plenty of reserves to make up the difference.

What is the easiest way to check out a fixed-rate annuity (existing contract or contemplated purchase)?

The Annuity Review Board provides detailed information regarding annuities and the insurance companies that issue them. For more information, telephone (619) 953-0599.

CHAPTER 6

The Intricacies of Variable Annuities

As the name implies, variable annuities offer you a variety of options. This chapter will explore these different investment options. The next chapter will show you how an annuity can be structured for withdrawals of principal and interest while still guaranteeing that the remaining investment will grow back to its original value. But before we go on, let us consider the range of opportunities and features that variable annuities afford.

Variable annuities were first introduced in the United States in the early 1950s. One of the best-known variable annuities is the College Retirement and Equities Fund (CREF). At the end of 1991 it was estimated that over $200 billion was invested in variable annuities and there were well over 8 million contract owners.

Why Choose a Variable Annuity?

If someone offers you a guaranteed competitive rate of return and complete security of principal at all times—in short, a fixed-rate annuity—why would you think twice about another investment that provides neither a guarantee of principal (at least not until death) nor rate of return? The answer is inflation.

When you invest in a government, corporate, or municipal bond, either directly or indirectly through a mutual fund, you are investing in something that is referred to as a fixed-rate instrument.

You are loaning your money to someone else or to some entity in return for a certain rate of return. Fixed-rate instruments would be great if we lived in a world of fixed-rate expenses.

It would be nice if the price of housing, rent, groceries, movie tickets, postage, clothes, and gasoline never increased. By investing all of your money in fixed-rate instruments, you are fooling yourself. In a sense, you are saying, "Inflation does not apply to me. I am unaffected by its cumulative effect."

If inflation averages 6% for a dozen years, the price of goods and services will have doubled by year 13. For millions of Americans, the cost of goods and services they purchase has escalated at a rate much higher than that. Of the families that can afford the American dream, both spouses work to own a home in most cases. How can you continue to maintain your current standard of living without some type of inflation hedge?

The more an investment outperforms inflation, the riskier it becomes. So, before you rush out and put all of your money in investments that are considered inflation hedges, first determine your risk level. No matter how much inflation bothers you, there is always a price to pay for investments that have the potential for growing at rates far above guaranteed accounts. That price can be some sleepless nights due to the increased volatility of your investment.

Investment Options

There are various investment options available to variable annuity investors. As you will see, each category provides the potential for certain rewards and risk.

Aggressive Growth

The investment objective of aggressive growth portfolios is maximum capital gains. Such funds usually invest in the common stock of very young companies and tend to stay fully invested over the market cycle. Sometimes these portfolios, or subaccounts of an annuity, will use leverage, and some may engage in trading stock options or index futures.

Aggressive growth portfolios typically provide low income distributions. This is because they tend to be fully invested in common stocks that pay small or no cash dividends. A small or nonexisting dividend stream is unimportant for the annuity investor since tax consequences are not an immediate concern. A high turnover rate results in a large capital gain liability for the mutual fund investor, but not for the annuity investor who has opted for deferred growth.

Many aggressive growth subaccounts concentrate their assets in just a few industries or segments of the market. Their degree of diversification may not be as great as other types of funds. These investment strategies result in increased risk. Thus, they tend to perform better than the overall market during bull markets but fare worse during bear markets.

In general, long-term investors who need not be concerned with monthly or yearly variation in investment return will find aggressive growth investments rewarding. Because of the extreme volatility of return, however, risk-averse investors with a short-term investment horizon may find that these funds can be offset by a greater allocation of an investor's total assets to a relatively risk-free investment, such as a money market fund. During prolonged market declines, aggressive growth funds can sustain severe declines in net asset value.

Table 6.1 shows how the entire aggressive growth category of variable annuities has performed against the S&P 500 over the past one-, three-, five-, and ten-year periods, ending December 31, 1991. The category "aggressive growth mutual funds" is shown for comparison purposes.

There is over $2 billion invested in aggressive growth subaccounts. The average portfolio is $59 million in size. At the beginning of 1992, there were 34 variable annuity subaccounts that were classified as "aggressive growth." Only one of these accounts is at least 10 years old. There are nine aggressive growth portfolios that have been around for five to nine years and only 21 that have existed for three to four years.

Growth

Growth accounts are typically more stable than aggressive growth portfolios. They generally do not engage in speculative tactics such

Table 6.1 *Performance of Variable Annuities Against S&P 500*

	1 Year	3 Years	5 Years	10 Years
Aggressive Growth	47.3%	21.8%	13.9%	13.4%
S&P 500	30.4%	18.5%	15.3%	17.5%
Aggressive Growth Mutual Funds	46.0%	19.1%	13.2%	11.54%

as using financial leverage. They invest in growth-oriented firms that pay cash dividends. You are likely to find companies such as IBM, PepsiCo, and McDonald's in the portfolios of growth accounts. The concentration of assets is not as limited as with aggressive growth subaccounts. Additionally, these accounts tend to move from fully invested to partially invested positions over a market cycle. They build up cash positions during uncertain market environments.

In general, variable annuities that invest in growth stocks tend to mirror the market during bull and bear markets. Some growth accounts have been able to perform relatively well during recent bear markets because their managers were able to change portfolio composition by a much greater degree or maintain much higher cash positions than aggressive growth managers. However, higher cash positions can cause these subaccounts to underperform aggressive growth positions during bull markets.

Growth portfolios can sustain severe declines during prolonged bear markets. Since some portfolio managers of growth accounts attempt to time the market over a longer cycle, switching these funds often may be counterproductive. Although market timing (attempting to gauge when the market is going to go up or down) is strongly discouraged, doing so with variable annuities will not trigger the taxable event that occurs with mutual fund market timing. Some people think that changing from, say, the XYZ Growth Mutual Fund to the XYZ Money Market Mutual Fund does not trigger a tax event since all activity takes place within the same "family." This is simply not true.

Table 6.2 shows how the entire growth category has performed against the S&P 500 over the past one-, three-, five-, and ten-year periods, ending December 31, 1991. The category "growth mutual funds" is shown for comparison purposes.

Table 6.2 *Performance of Growth Category Against S&P 500*

	1 Year	3 Years	5 Years	10 Years
Growth	34.8%	16.8%	12.8%	14.7%
S&P 500	30.4%	18.5%	15.3%	17.5%
Growth Mutual Funds	35.8%	17.2%	13.4%	15.3%

There is over $6 billion invested in growth subaccounts; the average portfolio is $59 million in size. At the beginning of 1992, there were 101 variable annuity subaccounts that were classified as "growth." There are 15 of these accounts that are at least 10 years old; 53 growth portfolios have been around for five to nine years, and 81 have existed for three to four years.

Growth and Income

Growth and income subaccounts generally invest in the common stocks and convertible securities of well-established, dividend-paying companies. Most of these companies attempt to provide shareholders with income along with long-term growth. One tends to find a high concentration of public utility common stocks and corporate convertible bonds in the portfolios of growth and income portfolios. The accounts also provide higher income distributions, less variation in return, and greater diversification than growth and aggressive growth positions. Equity income, income, and total return are subaccounts that have characteristics of growth and income portfolios.

Because of the high current income offered by these kinds of investments, prospective investors should keep the tax consequences in mind and use variable annuities whenever possible.

By selecting securities that have comparatively high yields, overall risk is reduced; dividends will help prop up the overall return of growth and income portfolios during negative market conditions. Growth and income is the most cautious U.S. stock play an investor can make.

Table 6.3 shows how the entire growth and income category has performed against the S&P 500 over the past one-, three-, five-, and ten-year periods, ending December 31, 1991. The cate-

Table 6.3 *Performance of Growth and Income Category Against S&P 500*

	1 Year	3 Years	5 Years	10 Years
Growth & Income	25.8%	13.2%	12.2%	16.8%
S&P 500	30.4%	18.5%	15.3%	17.5%
Growth and Income Mutual Funds	29.2%	15%	11.9%	14.7%

gory "growth and income mutual funds" is shown for comparison purposes.

There is over $5 billion invested in growth and income subaccounts; the average portfolio is $104 million in size. At the beginning of 1992, there were 48 variable annuity subaccounts that were classified as "growth and income." There is only one of these accounts that is at least 10 years old; there are 11 growth and income portfolios that have been around for five to nine years and only 37 that have existed for three to four years.

International Stocks

International subaccounts invest in securities of foreign companies only. They do not invest in U.S. stocks. Some portfolios specialize in certain regions, such as the Pacific Basin or Europe, and others invest worldwide. Global funds invest in both foreign and U.S. stocks.

International funds provide investors with added diversification. The most important factor when diversifying a portfolio is selecting assets that do not behave the same under similar economic scenarios. Within the United States, investors can diversify by selecting securities of firms in different industries. In the international realm, investors take the diversification process one step further by holding securities of different firms in different countries. The more independently these foreign markets move in relation to the U.S. market, the greater the diversification potential for the U.S. investor and, ultimately, the lower the risk.

In addition, international accounts overcome some of the difficulties investors would face in making foreign investments directly.

For instance, individuals would have to understand thoroughly the foreign brokerage process, international taxes, and various marketplaces and their economies, and they would have to be aware of currency fluctuation trends as well as have access to reliable financial information to make a proper investment decision. This can be a monumental task for the individual investor.

It is wise to consider investing abroad, since different economies experience prosperity and recession at different times. During the 1980s, foreign stocks were the number-one performing investment, averaging a compound return of over 22% per year versus 17% for U.S. stocks and 9% for residential real estate.

The economic outlook of foreign countries is the major factor in international investing. A secondary concern is the value of the U.S. dollar relative to foreign currencies. A strong or weak dollar can detract from or add to an international fund's overall performance. A strong dollar will lower a foreign portfolio's return; a weak dollar will enhance international performance. Trying to gauge the direction of any currency is as difficult as trying to figure out what the U.S. stock market will do tomorrow, next week, or next year.

Investors who do not wish to be subjected to currency swings may wish to use a variable annuity subaccount that practices currency hedging. Currency hedging is a type of "insurance policy" that pays off in the event of a strong U.S. dollar. Basically, the foreign or international fund that is being hurt by the dollar is making a killing in currency futures contracts. When properly handled, the gains in the futures contracts, the "insurance policy," offset most or all of security losses attributed to a strong dollar. Some people may think that buying currency contracts is risky business for the fund; it is not.

Like automobile insurance, currency hedging only pays off if there is an "accident"; that is, if the U.S. dollar increases in value against the currencies represented by the portfolio's securities. If the dollar remains level or decreases in value, so much the better; the foreign securities increase in value and the currency contracts become virtually worthless. The price of these contracts becomes a cost of doing business; just like car insurance, the protection is simply renewed. In the case of a currency contract, the contract expires and a new one is purchased, covering another period of time.

To understand how important currency hedging is on a risk-adjusted basis, consider how a foreign and U.S. stock portfolio fare against each other. Over the past 10 years, U.S. stocks have had a risk level of almost 16.5, as measured by standard deviation, versus just over 17 for foreign equities. Yet during this same period, foreign stocks have outperformed their U.S. counterparts by about 40% annually. Most readers would agree that the slightly greater risk of investing overseas is worth the vastly greater return.

The foregoing example becomes more dramatic when currency hedging is added to the foreign portfolio. The international risk level drops to a level of 13, while the U.S. level stays at almost 16.5. The returns for the foreign portfolio drop only slightly, due to the cost of buying "insurance." Nevertheless, the foreign equity portfolio still has annual returns a third greater than U.S. stocks. In short, a hedged foreign stock portfolio has 20% less risk than a U.S. stock fund while still providing a 33% greater return. This is truly the best of both worlds: less risk and greater returns.

If you were to construct a grid of the top-performing stock markets around the world, ranked first through fifth place and covering the past 12 years, you would have a total of 60 different slots. On this entire grid, the United States would appear only twice. In 1982 the United States had the second best-performing stock market in the world (+22%) and in 1991 it ranked third (+31%).

International subaccounts should be part of most people's portfolios. They provide superior returns and reduce overall portfolio risk. The real beauty of foreign equities shines through when they are combined with other categories of U.S. equities. According to a Stanford University study, your overall risk level is cut in half when a global portfolio of stocks is used instead of one based on U.S. issues alone. And, as already demonstrated, returns are greater when we look for opportunities worldwide instead of just domestically.

Table 6.4 shows how the entire international stock category has performed against the S&P 500 and the Morgan Stanley EAFE Index over the past one, three, five, and ten years, ending December 31, 1991. The EAFE index is the most commonly used measurement of foreign stock markets. The letters EAFE stand for Europe, Australia, and the Far East. This is a weighted index—Japan easily represents the largest component of this index. The category "international stock mutual funds" is shown for comparison purposes.

Table 6.4 Performance of International Stock Category Against S&P 500 and Morgan Stanley EAFE Index

	1 Year	3 Years	5 Years	10 Years
International Stock	12.6%	8.4%	n/a	n/a
S&P 500	30.4%	18.5%	15.3%	17.5%
EAFE Index (Foreign Stocks)	12.1%	−1.7%	8.7%	18%
International Stock Mutual Funds	13.8%	6.7%	8.8%	14.8%

There is over $1 billion invested in international stock accounts; the average portfolio is $33 million in size. At the beginning of 1992, there were 30 variable annuity subaccounts that were classified as "international stock." None of these portfolios has existed for five or more years. In fact, only 11 of these portfolios have been around for three to four years.

Balanced (Total Return)

Balanced or total return portfolios mix investments in common stocks, bonds, and convertible securities to decrease volatility and stabilize market swings.

As with growth and income accounts, balanced (total return) portfolios provide a high dividend yield which is sheltered from taxation within a variable annuity, but not within a mutual fund. Similarly, high tax-bracket investors who want to invest in these funds should consider using the tax-sheltered benefits of variable contracts.

The objective of balanced subaccounts is to provide both growth and income—taking advantage of market rises through stock holdings and providing income with bond holdings. The weighting of stocks versus bonds depends on the portfolio manager's perception of the stock market, interest rates, and risk levels.

Balanced portfolios offer neither the best nor worst of both worlds. They will often outperform the different categories of bond funds during bull markets, but suffer greater percentage losses during stock market declines. Conversely, when interest rates are on the rise, balanced accounts will typically decline less than bonds. When rates are falling, balanced subaccounts will also outperform a bond portfolio if stocks are doing well.

Balanced subaccounts are the perfect choice for the investor who wants a buffer against market volatility. The downside, of course, is that the portfolio will not rise as much as one that is fully invested in either market.

Table 6.5 shows how the entire balanced (total return) category has performed against the Shearson Lehman Brothers Government/Corporate Bond Index and the S&P 500 over the past one-, three-, five-, and ten-year periods, ending December 31, 1991. The Lehman Brothers index is the most commonly used way to measure the performance of domestic bonds. Both a bond and stock index were used for comparison purposes since balanced accounts are considered somewhat of a hybrid (comprised of approximately 30 to 70% in common stocks, with the remainder in corporate bonds and preferred securities). The category "balanced mutual funds" is shown for comparison purposes.

Balanced portfolios outperformed the bond index, since this category of annuities includes common and preferred stocks; the bond index did better over a 10-year horizon because the bond market experienced its best decade ever during the 1980s.

There is over $6 billion invested in balanced accounts; the average portfolio is $85.7 million in size. At the beginning of 1992, there were 70 variable annuity subaccounts that were classified as "balanced" or "total return." Only one of these portfolios has existed for 10 or more years. Fifteen total return portfolios have been

Table 6.5 *Performance of Balanced (Total Return) Category Against Shearson Lehman Brothers Government/Corporate Bond Index and S&P 500*

	1 Year	3 Years	5 Years	10 Years
Balanced	22.8%	13.1%	10.8%	12%
Government/Corporate Bond Index	16.1%	12.8%	9.6%	13.7%
S&P 500	30.4%	18.5%	15.3%	17.5%
Balanced Mutual Funds	25.1%	13.1%	10.4%	15.4%

around for five to nine years, and 43 have existed for three to four years.

Corporate Bonds

Corporate bond subaccounts invest in debt instruments issued by corporations. Bond portfolios have a wide range of maturities. The name of the portfolio will often indicate if it is comprised of short-term or medium-term obligations. If the name of the subaccount does not include the words *short-term* or *intermediate*, then the fund most likely invests in bonds that have average maturities over 15 years. The greater the maturity, the more the portfolio's unit price can change. There is an inverse relationship between interest rates and the value of a bond; when one moves up, the other goes down.

Since corporate and government bonds generate high interest payments, the ideal investment vehicle for holding such instruments is a variable annuity. The risk reduction that bonds provide (there have only been six years over the past 66 years in which both bonds and stocks declined), coupled with a tax-deferral benefit, make a strong case for owning these within a variable annuity.

Table 6.6 shows how the entire corporate bond category has performed against the Shearson Lehman Brothers Government/ Corporate Bond Index and the Consumer Price Index (CPI) over the past one-, three-, five-, and ten-year periods, ending December 31, 1991. The Lehman Brothers index is the most commonly used way to measure the performance of domestic bonds. The category "corporate bond mutual funds" is shown for comparison purposes.

Table 6.6 *Performance of Corporate Bond Category Against Shearson Lehman Brothers Corporate Bond Index and the Consumer Price Index (CPI)*

	1 Year	3 Years	5 Years	10 Years
Corporate	15.2%	10.4%	7.8%	11%
Corporate Bond Index	16.1%	12.8%	9.6%	13.7%
CPI (the Rate of Inflation)	3%	4.6%	4.5%	3.9%
Corporate Bond Mutual Funds	14.5%	11.4%	8.7%	13%

There is over $2 billion invested in corporate bond accounts; the average portfolio is $32 million in size. At the beginning of 1992, there were 62 variable annuity subaccounts that were classified as "corporate bond." Six of these portfolios have existed for 10 or more years. Thirty-four corporate subaccounts have been around for five to nine years, and 55 have existed for three to four years.

Government Bonds

Government bond subaccounts include both mortgage-backed securities, such as GNMAs and FNMAs, and U.S. Treasury obligations. Such portfolios are attractive to bond investors because they provide diversification and marketability, which are not as readily available in direct bond investments.

As with all bonds, governments have a wide range of maturities. Since bond subaccounts provide diversification, investors should invest in larger portfolios. As a result of economies of scale, large bond portfolios tend to operate more efficiently.

Due to the mortality cost charged by variable annuities (which averages just over 1% annually), it is best to minimize your bond subaccount holdings as much as possible. Expenses eat away at returns. So bond accounts would need to be held, on average, for at least 10 years to make them more worthwhile than a mutual fund or direct ownership. This issue is explained more fully in Chapter 9.

Table 6.7 shows how the entire government bond category has performed against the Shearson Lehman Brothers Government/ Corporate Bond Index and the Consumer Price Index (CPI) over the

Table 6.7 *Performance of Government Bond Category Against Shearson Lehman Brothers Government Bond Index and the Consumer Price Index (CPI)*

	1 Year	3 Years	5 Years	10 Years
Government Bond	14.6%	11.2%	7.9%	11.8%
Government Bond Index	15.3%	12.7%	9.4%	13.1%
CPI (the Rate of Inflation)	3%	4.6%	4.5%	3.9%
Government Bond Mutual Funds	13.7%	11.2%	8.2%	12.4%

past one-, three-, five-, and ten-year periods, ending December 31, 1991. The Lehman Brothers index is the most commonly used method to measure the performance of domestic bonds. The category "government bond mutual funds" is shown for comparison purposes.

There is over $2 billion invested in government bond accounts; the average portfolio is $50 million in size. At the beginning of 1992, there were 40 variable annuity subaccounts that were classified as "government bond." Only two government portfolios have existed for 10 or more years. Eleven government subaccounts have been around for five to nine years, and 19 have existed for three to four years.

High-Yield Bonds

These accounts generally invest in lower-rated debt instruments. Bonds are either characterized as "bank quality," also known as "investment grade," or "junk." Investment-grade bonds are those bonds that are either rated AAA, AA, A, or BAA. Junk bonds are those instruments rated less than BAA (ratings such as BB, B, CCC, CC, C, and D). High-yield bonds can offer investors higher returns due to the additional risk of default. High-yield bonds are subject to less interest-rate risk than regular corporate or government bonds. However, when the economy slows or people panic, these bonds can quickly drop in value. The high current income can only be sheltered in a retirement plan or variable annuity; a dividend and/or interest reinvestment program with a mutual fund does not minimize any taxes due.

The world of bonds is not black and white. There are several categories of high-yield bonds. The high end of the junk bond market, those debentures rated BBB and BB, has been able to withstand the general beating the junk bond market incurred during the late 1980s and early 1990. Moderate and conservative investors who want high-yield bonds as part of their portfolio should focus on subaccounts that have a high percentage of their assets in higher-rated bonds, BB or better.

Table 6.8 shows how the entire high-yield bond category has performed against the Shearson Lehman Brothers Corporate Bond Index and the Consumer Price Index (CPI) over the past one-,

Table 6.8 *Performance of High-yield Bond Category Against Shearson Lehman Brothers Corporate Bond Index and Consumer Price Index (CPI)*

	1 Year	3 Years	5 Years	10 Years
High-yield Bond	34.9%	7.3%	6.4%	n/a
Corporate Bond Index	18.5%	13.1%	10.2%	15.3%
CPI (the Rate of Inflation)	3%	4.6%	4.5%	3.9%
High-yield Bond Mutual Funds	35.3%	6.1%	6.1%	11.6%

three-, five-, and ten-year periods, ending December 31, 1991 (in this case, such a comparison is rough at best and not necessarily fair). The category "high-yield bond funds" is shown for comparison purposes.

There is over $1 billion invested in high-yield bond accounts; the average portfolio is $28.5 million in size. At the beginning of 1992, there were 35 variable annuity subaccounts that were classified as "high yield." No high-yield portfolios have existed for 10 or more years. Twelve junk bond subaccounts have been around for five to nine years, and 27 have existed for three to four years.

Global and International Bonds

International bond portfolios invest in foreign fixed-income securities. These fixed-income obligations are denominated in various currencies such as francs, pounds, yen, and deutsche marks. Of course, fixed-income markets do involve some risk, which can be reduced through global diversification.

Countries move in different economic cycles, and so do the capital gain prospects of the bonds issued in those countries. At any one time, a certain country may offer the highest returns. But as global economic cycles turn, a different country may then hold out the greatest opportunities. International bond portfolios have outperformed their U.S. counterparts over the past 5, 10, 15, 20, and 25 years. Global diversification also reduces the investor's risk level. And, although there are not many variable annuities that have international or global bond subaccounts, they should be sought out.

Prospective investors need to be aware of the potential changes in the value of the foreign currency relative to the U.S. dollar when investing in international subaccounts. For example, if you were to invest in Australian dollar-denominated bonds that had a current yield of 15% and the Aussie currency appreciated 12% against the U.S. dollar, your total return for the year would be 27%. Conversely, if the Australian dollar declined by 20% against the U.S. dollar, your total return would be −5%.

Global portfolios invest in securities issued all over the world, including the United States. A global account usually invests in bonds issued by stable governments from a handful of countries. Management tries to avoid purchasing foreign government debt instruments from politically or economically unstable nations.

Global bond accounts seek higher interest rates no matter where the search may take them. Inclusion in the portfolio depends on management's perception of interest rates, the country's projected currency strength against the U.S. dollar, and the country's political and economic stability.

Since foreign markets do not necessarily move in tandem with U.S. markets, each country represents varying investment opportunities at different times. The current value of the world bond market is estimated at close to $8 trillion. Half of this marketplace is comprised of U.S. bonds. Japan ranks second, taking up 20% of the pie. Variable annuities that invest in global securities, particularly those that have a high concentration in foreign issues, are an excellent risk-reduction tool that the vast majority of investors should utilize.

Table 6.9 shows how the entire global bond category has performed against the Shearson Lehman Brothers Government/Corporate Bond Index and the Consumer Price Index (CPI) over the past one, three, five, and ten years, ending December 31, 1991. The Lehman Brothers index is the most commonly used way to measure the performance of domestic bonds. This form of comparison is only rough because the category "global bonds" may only include modest amounts of U.S. bonds. Nevertheless, you will get a good sense of how one type of bond has performed against another. The category "international bond mutual funds" is shown for comparison purposes.

There is over $141 million invested in global bond accounts; the average portfolio is $10 million in size. At the beginning of 1992,

Table 6.9 *Performance of Global Bond Category Against Shearson Lehman Brothers Government/Corporate Bond Index and Consumer Price Index (CPI)*

	1 Year	3 Years	5 Years	10 Years
Global Bond	13%	10.6%	11.9%	n/a
Government/Corporate Bond Index	16.1%	12.8%	9.6%	13.7%
CPI (the Rate of Inflation)	3%	4.6%	4.5%	3.9%
International Bond Mutual Funds	11.3%	9.6%	9.3%	14.7%

there were 14 variable annuity subaccounts that were classified as "global bond." None of these portfolios has existed for 10 or more years. In fact, only three of these portfolios have been around for five to nine years, and only eight have existed for three to four years.

Specialty Portfolios

Variable annuities that are described as sector or "specialty" plays invest primarily in the stocks of a single industry. The current top performers in this area are those subaccounts that invest heavily in real estate securities. However, the category also includes utility stocks, natural resources, and precious metals.

This category should not represent more than 15% of your total holdings. This limitation is recommended for two reasons. First, by opting for a specialty or sector account, you are tying investment management's hands. Their ability to find worthy stocks is limited by prospectus to a certain industry. If this industry or sector is not performing well, the subaccount will not do well either—no matter how skilled the management. Second, sector plays are considered very risky. The entire subaccount is prone to the fortune or misfortune of a particular industry. Equally important, if you were to review the performance of all sector and specialty portfolios combined (e.g., add up the performance of metals, natural resource subaccounts, etc.), you would find that you now have the worst of both worlds: substandard performance and above-average risk.

Specialty portfolios do provide some benefits, however. First, these accounts allow you to invest in, say, real estate without going through the trouble of buying and managing your own properties. Second, sector plays, when combined with a well-considered portfolio, can actually reduce overall volatility. Alone they are quite risky, but when combined with other categories such as growth, international, and high yield, this category can lower your total risk.

Table 6.10 shows how the entire specialty category has performed against the S&P 500 and U.S. Treasury Bills over the past one-, three-, five-, and ten-year periods, ending December 31, 1991. The category "specialty—natural resources mutual funds" is shown for comparison purposes since this is the type of specialty portfolio represented by the variable annuity subaccount index.

There is over $237 million invested in specialty subaccounts; the average portfolio is $10.7 million in size. At the beginning of 1992, there were 22 variable annuity subaccounts that were classified as "specialty." None of these accounts has existed for five or more years; only eight have been around for three to four years.

Monitoring Performance

One of the nice features of annuities is that you can always find out how well your investment is performing. Most annuity companies have toll-free telephone numbers you can call to find out your investment results. Several companies have an automated service that can give you information—including account balances—24 hours a day, seven days a week.

Table 6.10 *Performance of Specialty Category Against S&P 500 and U.S. Treasury Bills*

	1 Year	3 Years	5 Years	10 Years
Specialty Portfolios	15.4%	5.9%	n/a	n/a
S&P 500	30.4%	18.5%	15.3%	17.5%
U.S. Treasury Bills	5.3%	6.9%	6.7%	7.5%
Specialty—Natural Resources Mutual Funds	6.8%	7.9%	8.4%	8.3%

In addition to contacting the insurance company, performance can also be monitored by subscribing to one of several periodicals. *Barron's*, a weekly publication, lists unit values of several hundred variable annuities. *The Wall Street Journal* has also increased its coverage of annuities and periodically runs performance figures on some of the best- and worst-performing variable annuities.

For serious variable annuity investors, there are several professional monitoring services. One of the best is *The VARDS Report*, a monthly publication. An annual subscription costs $698, which includes contract information and outlines all products followed. VARDS is published by Financial Planning Resources, Inc., P.O. Box 161998, Miami, Florida 33116. For a free sample copy, write or telephone (305)252-4600. The *Lipper Variable Insurance Products Performance Analysis Service*, published by Lipper Analytical Securities Corporation, contains performance figures on variable life insurance as well as variable annuities. For a sample copy, write to Lipper Analytical Services, Inc., 47 Maple St., Summit, New Jersey 07901, or telephone (201)273-2772.

More complete information is provided for these and other services in Appendix A, "Sources of Additional Information."

No Junk Bond or Real Estate Worries

During the past few years, stories have emerged about the amount of junk bonds and poor real estate investments held by several insurance companies. With *fixed-rate* annuities, the monies you invest are commingled with the insurance company's general portfolio. This general portfolio includes the good and bad. In theory, your account could be compromised either temporarily or permanently by poor investment choices. Two insurance companies, Skandia and Hartford, maintain separate accounts for their fixed-rate annuity contracts. Such separation means that investors do not need to lose sleep over whether or not the issuing company falls into financial trouble. The commingling can also be avoided by investing in variable contracts.

One of the advantages of a variable annuity is that if the insurance company runs into financial problems, funds (because they are held in separate subaccounts) are beyond the reach of the company's creditors. Variable annuities are also subject to regulation by the SEC, the National Association of Securities Dealers (NASD), and state regulatory bodies. Fixed-rate annuities are regulated by each state's insurance commission.

Dollar-Cost Averaging

Some investors believe that the market will go down as soon as they get in. We call this the "kiss of death" syndrome. For these people, and anyone concerned with reducing risk, the solution is *dollar-cost averaging* (DCA).

Dollar-cost averaging is a simple yet effective way to reduce risk, whether you are investing in stocks or bonds. The premise behind DCA is that if several purchases of a variable annuity are made over an extended period of time, the unpredictable highs and lows will "average out." The investor ends up with buying some units at a comparatively low price, and others at perhaps a much higher price.

Dollar-cost averaging assumes that investors are willing to sacrifice the possibility of having bought all of their units at the lowest price in return for knowing that they did not also buy every unit at the highest price. In short, we are willing to accept a compromise, a sort of risk-reduction decision.

Dollar-cost averaging is based on investing a fixed amount of money in a given annuity at specific intervals. Typically, an investor will add a few hundred dollars at the beginning of each month into the XYZ variable annuity. Dollar-cost averaging works best if you invest and continue to invest on a preestablished schedule, *regardless of price fluctuations.* You will be buying more units when the price is down than when it is up. Most investors do not mind buying units when prices are increasing, since this means that their existing units are also going up. When this program is followed, losses during market declines are limited, while the ability to participate in good markets is maintained.

Another advantage of DCA is that it increases the likelihood that you will follow an investment program. Like other aspects of our life, it is important to have goals and objectives. An example of DCA is given in Figure 6.1.

Period (1)	Price of Security (2)	Number of Units Bought with $1,000 (3)	Total Units Owned (4)	Total Amount Invested (5)	Current Value of Units (2) × (4) (6)	Net Gain or Loss Percentage (6)/(5) (7)
1	$100	10.0	10.0	$1,000	$1,000	0
2	80	12.5	22.5	2,000	1,800	−10.0
3	70	14.3	36.8	3,000	2,576	−14.1
4	60	16.7	53.5	4,000	3,210	−19.7
5	50	20.0	73.5	5,000	3,675	−26.5
6	70	14.3	87.8	6,000	6,146	+2.4
7	80	12.5	100.3	7,000	8,024	+14.6
8	100	10.0	110.3	8,000	11,030	+37.9

FIGURE 6.1 Example of Dollar-Cost Averaging ($1,000 Invested per Period).

Systematic Withdrawals

A systematic withdrawal plan (SWP) allows you to have a check for a specified amount sent monthly or quarterly to you, or anyone you designate, from your annuity. There is no charge for this service. This method of getting monthly checks is ideal for the income-oriented investor. It is also a risk reduction technique—a type of dollar-cost averaging in *reverse*.

When the market is low, the number of units being liquidated will be higher than when the market is high. If you need $500 a month and the portfolio's price is $25.00 per unit, 20 units must be liquidated; if the price per unit is $20.00, 25 units must be sold.

Figure 6.2 shows an example of an SWP from the Investment Company of America, a conservative growth and income mutual fund. Similar results would occur if a variable annuity were used, but variable accounts have not existed for this lengthy a period. The example assumes an initial investment of $100,000 in the fund at its inception, in early 1934. A greater or smaller amount could be used. The example shows what happens to the investor's principal over a 57-year period of time. It assumes that $9,000 is withdrawn from the fund each year. At the end of the first year, the $9,000 is *increased by 5% each year* to offset the effects of inflation, which averaged less than 4% during this 57-year period.

Compare the example in Figure 6.1 to what would have happened if the money had been placed in an average fixed-income account at a bank. The $100,000 depositor who took out just $9,000 each year would be in a far different situation. The original $100,000 would be fully depleted by the end of 1948—all the principal and interest payments could not keep up with an annual withdrawal of $9,000.

The difference between ICA and the savings account is over $7 million (withdrawals and principal). This difference becomes even more astounding when you consider that the bank depositor's withdrawals were not increasing each year to offset the affects of inflation. The interest rates used in this example came from the *U.S. Savings & Loan League Fact Book*.

Next time some broker or banker tells you that you should be buying bonds or CDs for current income, tell him or her about a systematic withdrawal plan, which is designed to maximize your income and offset something the CD, T-bill, and bond sellers never mention: inflation. This is a program that can easily be used with annuities as well as mutual funds.

THE INVESTMENT COMPANY OF AMERICA (ICA)		
Initial investment: $100,000		Annual withdrawals: $9,000 (9%)
First check: 12/31/34		Withdrawals annually increase: 5%

Date	Amount Withdrawn	Value of Remaining Shares
12/31/34	$9,000	$112,000
12/31/35	$9,450	$196,000
12/31/40	$12,000	$165,000
12/31/45	$15,000	$277,000
12/31/50	$20,000	$250,000
12/31/55	$25,000	$463,000
12/31/60	$32,000	$595,000
12/31/65	$41,000	$890,000
12/31/70	$52,000	$988,000
12/31/75	$67,000	$907,000
12/31/80	$85,000	$1,369,000
12/31/85	$108,000	$2,408,000
12/31/86	$114,000	$2,818,000
12/31/87	$119,000	$2,852,000
12/31/88	$125,000	$3,107,000
12/31/89	$132,000	$7,388,000
12/31/90	$138,000	$3,777,000
12/31/91	$145,000	$4,617,000

FIGURE 6.2 **Systematic Withdrawal Plan Example.**

Commonly Asked Questions

What do I purchase with my variable annuity premium?

Your premium usually purchases accumulation units in the insurance company's account, which is maintained separately from the company's regular portfolio of investments. This separate account, in turn, purchases shares in securities portfolios established and administered for the variable annuity. In this sense, accumulation units are similar to shares in a mutual fund.

Like mutual fund shares, each unit's value or "price" is determined by the value of the portfolio divided by the number of units outstanding. Each unit represents a share of the total worth of the portfolio. For example, assume that a $10 million portfolio has 1 million accumulation units and each unit has a current value of $10. If the portfolio appreciates to $12 million, the unit value rises to $12 each. Divide your premium by the unit value at the time you invest to approximate the number of units you will purchase.

Most annuities also let you allocate funds to a fixed-account option that is part of the insurer's regular portfolio and guarantees a minimum interest rate.

What happens once I have purchased accumulation units?

The underlying securities have the potential to earn interest, dividends, and/or capital gains, which may be reinvested to earn still more income. This tax-deferred compounding—earning current income on past income without paying taxes until later—allows the value of the accumulation units to grow considerably faster than with a comparable taxable investment.

What types of securities do variable annuity portfolios contain?

The majority of variable annuities provide you with a choice of portfolios of stocks, bonds, and/or money market instruments. You allocate your money to purchase accumulation units in different portfolios, depending on how aggressive or conservative you wish to be.

Do I have to make all of the investment decisions?

Maintaining a balance between stocks, bonds, and money market instruments can be tough. If you would prefer experts to make the choices, an asset allocation portfolio might be best for you. Professional managers view current market and economic conditions to determine the best mix of investments for achieving a portfolio's objective at any point in time. The objective of an asset allocation portfolio usually is to provide a predetermined level of total return consistent with long-term preservation of capital.

Can I change my investment portfolio mix whenever I wish?

Yes. But investors should remember warnings about market timing. It is best to leave monies vested for a longer period of time to achieve maximum growth. However, there are usually no restrictions on subaccount switching within a variable annuity.

CHAPTER 7

Split Annuities: The Best of Both Worlds

This chapter shows you an investment strategy that you can use with either a variable or fixed-rate annuity. It shows how a certain percentage of principal and interest can be withdrawn while the remaining investment grows and compounds, eventually equaling the original amount invested.

The proper name for this concept is a *split annuity*. The contract owner simply divides the value of the account into two parts: One part is distributed while the other part remains intact, growing. The split annuity can be done with either a fixed or variable account, but only the fixed-rate annuity can make the guarantee of complete restoration within a set period of time.

Split annuities are used as a means of maximizing income while preserving wealth. In addition, like any annuitization program, they offer a tax advantage.

How a Split Annuity Works

The following example illustrates how a split annuity works: Begin with a $100,000 original investment. Place $54,602 into a fixed-rate annuity that guarantees a 7.80% rate of return for the next eight years. Place the remaining $45,398 into an annuity that is immediately annuitized for the same eight years. By using guaranteed accounts, the $54,602 will be worth exactly $100,000 in eight years.

The annuitized portion provides a monthly income of $575.06; $472.90 of it is not subject to income taxes (due to the exclusion ratio discussed in the previous chapter). In this way, you get income from one portion of your annuity, and the rest of the annuity continues to grow without suffering a loss from distribution.

An Alternative Approach

Would you be interested in an investment that offers the appreciation potential of the stock and bond markets and guarantees your principal when held to maturity? With the following variation, you can "play the market" with peace of mind guaranteed.

Assume an initial investment of $100,000. For guaranteed return of your original investment in eight years, invest $54,602 in the fixed account. Assuming an eight-year locked-in rate of 7.8%, this amount would grow to $100,000.

For potential capital growth and appreciation, invest the $45,398 balance in a variable account—the return on which is not guaranteed—for the same eight-year period. Based on the past performance of a conservative variable annuity portfolio comprised of high-quality stocks and bonds, the balance would grow to $106,000.

Who Should Use Split Annuities?

Anyone who needs current income, needs a tax break, and wants a guarantee at the end of a specific period should consider split annuities.

The next chapter provides a brief intermission from the world of annuities. It shows how to calculate how fast money doubles or quadruples. You can use this formula with any type of investment, including fixed-rate and variable annuities, and you do not need a calculator or computer to use it.

Commonly Asked Questions

Can the monthly payment of a split annuity change?

Yes. The amount you receive each month will fluctuate with the performance of the securities portfolios you have selected. There will be no variation or unknowns if fixed-rate annuities are used instead.

What's the difference between a split annuity and an immediate annuity?

The split annuity is designed to restore principal. An immediate annuity only capitalizes on short-term performance. There are no guarantees with immediate annuities in terms of performance (unless fixed-rate accounts are used), while split annuities can offer such a feature. In addition, split annuities are usually long-term investment vehicles, while immediate annuities vary from just a few years to a lifetime.

Is the variable or fixed option better under a split annuity scenario?

This depends on market conditions and whether or not you want a guarantee at the end of a specific investment period. Total return potential on the variable is greater than the fixed, but the guarantees are not there.

Can I change the amount destined for liquidation or growth?

As with all annuities, the distribution is flexible (prior to annuitization). If you do not need as much income, the payout provision provided in your contract can be amended. Conversely, if you find that your payout is not enough, the split annuity can be weighted more heavily for income as opposed to growth. You only become locked in on any portion you annuitize.

CHAPTER 8

How Fast Will Your Money Grow?

You should know the expected earnings of any investment and what will happen to those earnings if you reinvest them. You know that if earnings are reinvested for a long enough period of time, the investment will double in value. The question, of course, is "How long must I wait?"

The Rule of 72

The Rule of 72 is a simple formula you can use to see how fast one dollar will grow to two dollars (or, for example, how quickly it will take $23,000 to grow and compound to $46,000). The equation is comprised of a quick division problem. Take the assumed, projected, or guaranteed rate of return from an investment and divide it into the number 72. The resulting number, or answer, shows you how many years it will take an investment to double in value.

For example, suppose you are looking at a variable annuity that has averaged 18% over the past several years and you want to know how long it will take your $25,000 to grow to $50,000. To find out, take 18, the projected rate of return, and divide it into 72. Eighteen goes into 72 four times. This means that $25,000 will grow to $50,000 in four years. If you decide on a fixed-rate annuity that has a locked-in rate of 10%, it would take 7.2 years for your $25,000 to double in value to $50,000 (10 divided into 72 equals 7.2).

Comprehending Inflation

The Rule of 72 also shows us something about the terrible effects of inflation. It shows us how quickly the purchasing power of a dollar, yen, peso, or franc can be cut in half. For example, if you assume a steady 6% average annual rate of inflation, a dollar will only buy 50 cents worth of goods and services at the end of 12 years (6 divided into 72 equals 12). At the end of the second 12-year period, the purchasing power will be cut in half again. Thus, one dollar shrinks to 50 cents and then drops to 25 cents in real value. In other words, at the end of the first 12 years, it will take two dollars to buy what you could have bought previously for one dollar. After another 12-year period, it will take four dollars to equal the same purchasing power of the original dollar 24 years previously.

Since it is extremely likely that inflation will stay with us for the remainder of our lifetimes, it is important that you recognize its cruel effects and try to safeguard against a declining lifestyle. Chapter 6 discussed several investment options that have proven to be excellent hedges against inflation.

Doubling Power

No matter how old you are, your investments can only double in value so many times. The younger you are, the more doubling periods you will enjoy. Every investor's primary goal should be for the *growth* portion of his or her portfolio to double as many times as possible before a certain event occurs (death, retirement, children reaching college age, etc.). Equally important, the money must be in investments that have an acceptable risk level.

Many people, particularly young singles and couples, postpone building a portfolio in lieu of other perceived priorities, such as buying a new car, boat, or electronic equipment. They believe that they can begin saving "next year." Usually, next year comes and goes and no investment strategy has been implemented. In fact, what usually happens is that five or ten years lapse before any kind of plan is put into place.

People who postpone starting an investment portfolio do not know how much even a few years' delay will cost them later. For example, suppose you and your neighbor each have $100,000 to invest. With some skill and a little luck, you both feel that you can average 14% per year for many years to come. The only difference between you and your neighbor is that you invest your money now and he waits five years to make a commitment. At the end of approximately 20 years, your $100,000 in a tax-deferred variable annuity is worth $1,600,000. By waiting five years, your neighbor, who also invested in a tax-deferred annuity, missed a doubling period. His $100,000 grows to only $800,000. The five-year delay cost your neighbor exactly $800,000.

The calculations in the previous example were easy to perform. According to the Rule of 72, if one averages 14%, money doubles every 5.1 years (72 divided by 14 equals 5.142 years). If, in this example, it takes 5.1 years for money to double, how many doubling periods are there? There are approximately four doubling periods in a 20-year time horizon (20 divided by 5.1 equals about 4, thus 4 doubling periods). During the first doubling period, $100,000 grew to $200,000; during the second doubling period, $200,000 grew to $400,000. The third doubling period saw $400,000 grow to $800,000 and the final doubling period saw $800,000 compound to $1,600,000.

Your neighbor got the same rate of return you did, but for a shorter period of time. His compounding lasted for only 15 years, not 20 years. And, as the previous paragraph points out, this means he only received three doublings: $100,000 grew to $200,000, then $200,000 compounded to $400,000, and finally $400,000 doubled a third time to $800,000. There is certainly nothing wrong with $800,000, but it is only half as good as $1,600,000. It is doubtful your neighbor would have procrastinated if he had known the delay would cost him $800,000.

Delaying your investment portfolio means that you will be losing out on part or all of one or more extra doubling periods. It will not be the first or second doubling period that you miss, when $10,000 grows to $20,000 and then $20,000 grows to $40,000. The delay will cost you part or all of the last one or two doublings, after the $40,000 continues to compound to $80,000 and then to $160,000. It will be the jump from $160,000 to $320,000 and then part or all of the doubling when $320,000 grows to $640,000.

Contribute Early

Another way to examine the cost of procrastination is by showing what happens if you have two investors who make periodic contributions of the same dollar amount. Assume that the first investor, age 35, referred to as the "early contributor," invests $5,000 in a variable annuity each year for the next 10 years (a total of $50,000 contributed over a decade).

The second investor, also age 35, referred to as the "procrastinator," postpones making any investment until the eleventh year, when he is now age 45 (after the early contributor has invested a total of $50,000). The procrastinator, in an attempt to catch up, invests $7,500 every year for 21 years. At the end of 21 years, the procrastinator has invested a total of $157,500.

Assuming both investors each get a 12% annual compound rate of growth, the early contributor will have $1,061,726 at age 65, while the procrastinator ends up with $682,269 when he reaches age 65 (even though the procrastinator made increased contributions and contributed for 11 more years than the early contributor).

A final twist on the preceding example: Assuming a continued 12% growth rate, the procrastinator will never catch up with the early contributor. This is true even if the procrastinator continues to add $7,500 each year to the portfolio and the early contributor invests only $5,000 for the first 10 years, never making another contribution.

Doubling Your Retirement Income

The example shown in Figure 8.1 shows two different investors planning for retirement. One investor relies on traditional investments that are fully taxable each year. The other investor gets the same rate of return but enjoys the long-term rewards of tax deferral—rewards that benefit her long after retirement begins.

The Final Word

Prior to his death, Albert Einstein was asked what was the most amazing thing he had ever seen in his long career. His reply was, "Compound interest!"

The next chapter compares and contrasts annuities to mutual funds. Mutual funds are owned by one out of every four households. Over $1.5 trillion is invested in the mutual fund industry. In the next

12% Assumed Growth Rate	12% Assumed Growth Rate
− 33% Tax Rate	− Pay No Current Tax
= 8% Net Growth Rate	= 12% Net Growth Rate
72 ÷ 8% = 9 Years to Double Your Money	72 ÷ 12% = 6 Years to Double Your Money

Taxable Investment	Age	Tax-Deferred Investment
$50,000	50	$50,000
	56	$100,000
$100,000	59	
	62	$200,000
$200,000	68	$400,000

Now at retirement, earn and
spend 12% from each investment.

Annual Taxable Income:
$24,000 versus $48,000.

Which would you prefer?
$24,000 a year during retirement or $48,000 a year?

*The tax-deferred investment was able to provide 100% more
money—twice as much income.*

FIGURE 8.1 **Investment Comparison Example.**

chapter we will compare these two giants and see which one emerges
as the victor.

Commonly Asked Questions

How much should my premium (investment) be for retirement purposes?

You determine your premium (subject to minimum requirements).
Your decision will be based on three major factors:

1. How much income you will need in addition to social security, pension income, and other investments

2. Whether you will need income only for yourself, or for someone else also
3. How much you can afford to pay.

Your financial planning professional can help sort out these factors.

Does the Rule of 72 work for other investments?

Yes. When comparing how fast it takes an asset to double in value, keep in mind that you must consider the annual tax ramifications of the investment, unless it is sheltered within a retirement account or annuity.

I know I should invest early, but what if I can't afford to?

Then don't. Basic needs must be met before any investment program should be considered. However, you may have some discretionary income and not know it. Do you need to eat out every night or buy a new car every year? Your financial adviser can often uncover some spending patterns that can be altered to incorporate a savings and/or investment program.

How can I use the Rule of 72 with a variable annuity if rates of return vary?

The best you can do is estimate. Variable annuity performance can be measured with an average annual rate of return. While there is no guarantee that past performance will equal future performance, an average rate of return is the best measuring stick available.

Is it worth investing even if I don't have any doubling periods left in my lifetime?

Doubling periods are only one consideration in annuity (or any other) investing. Other annuity features may outweigh the benefits of investment returns over time.

CHAPTER 9

Annuities Versus Mutual Funds

Common Features

Both annuities and mutual funds are easy to invest in and monitor. Both offer professional management. Both offer outstanding track records and several different investment options. Money can be added to or taken out of either investment at any time; both types of investment vehicles offer dollar-cost averaging (a way to invest in the stock and/or bond markets without buying in at a high point) and systematic withdrawal programs. Annuities and mutual funds can be started with as little as $250. Part or all of the investment can be moved within the family of investment options offered by the mutual fund group or variable annuity contract.

Differences

Despite these common traits, annuities and mutual funds have a number of differences, including (1) commissions, (2) taxation, (3) performance, (4) withdrawal options, (5) investment choices, and (6) safety.

Commissions

Most mutual funds charge some type of commission, ranging from 1 to 8.5%. This commission is normally subtracted from your investment. Thus, a $5,000 investment in a mutual fund may mean that only $4,575 is going to work for you ($5,000 minus 8.5% equals $4,575). This means that you may have to make close to a 10% return on your money before you break even.

Fixed and variable annuities do not charge a commission to the investor. Whenever you invest in any annuity, 100% of your investment goes to work for you immediately. The same is true for any additional contributions made to your initial investment. For example, if you start off with $10,000 and the account grows by 20% during the year, your account is now worth $12,000.

With *all* of your money earning interest or growing, you can reap a higher rate of return. The 1 to 8.5% commission you might have paid to invest in a mutual fund could have been earning interest or growing in an annuity. In time, this modest amount can really make a difference.

Taxation

When you own a mutual fund, there are three potential sources of income tax: (1) the dividends or interest thrown off by the securities in the portfolio, (2) the capital gains realized whenever the fund manager sells stocks or bonds, or (3) the resulting profits when you sell shares of your mutual fund or make changes within the mutual fund family. You cannot control the first two situations; you are at the mercy of the fund. It would be ridiculous to think that you could tell a fund not to accept a stock's dividend or the interest payment from a bond. It would be equally absurd to think that you could tell a fund manager not to sell so many stocks or bonds because you were in a high tax bracket and wanted to minimize your tax bill for the year.

The only tax aspect of a mutual fund that you can control is your own purchase and sale of fund shares. You decide when part or all of the account should be liquidated or switched from the XYZ bond fund to the XYZ stock or money market fund. Unfortunately, all of these events trigger a taxable event. Some people believe that if they switch their money among different funds within the same family, this does not result in any taxation. In fact, the IRS considers this to be a sale and subsequent purchase—a taxable event.

When you invest in a fixed-rate or variable annuity, money grows and compounds tax deferred indefinitely. The only time you pay income tax is when a withdrawal is made. And you only pay taxes on those withdrawals that are considered accumulated growth or interest. Monies received that are considered a return of principal are not taxable.

As economic conditions change, opportunities arise, or personal temperaments change, you may wish to become more conservative or aggressive in your investment program. In an annuity, assets can be repositioned to accommodate such changes *without* triggering a tax event. Thus, you no longer face the dilemma of wanting to sell a security whose future performance no longer looks good (e.g., a stock or mutual fund you bought for $10 a share which went up to $40 a share and is now sliding downward). With an annuity, you can freeze your gains or limit your losses at any time without having to pay taxes.

To understand how costly such a decision can be, consider an actual example: an international stock fund offered by the American Funds Group. This fund, EuroPacific Growth, began operating in 1984. Since its inception on April 16, 1984 through May 31, 1992, the fund had an average compound annual growth rate of 17.9%. An initial investment of $100,000 grew to $382,133. During this seven-year period, fund shareholders received $28,914 in dividends and $66,309 in taxable capital gains (both of these figures are low for an equity or stock fund).

Furthermore, taxes on the dividends, based on a 33% tax bracket, were $9,542. Capital gains tax, which has a maximum rate of 28%, came to $18,567. These two figures, which total $28,109, represent how much an investor would have paid in taxes during the seven years. An annuity owner would have paid zero. During this same period, the fund also appreciated $186,910. If the investor decided to move money out of the fund at the end of this period, the 28% capital gains tax incurred would result in $52,335 more in taxes. The tough question is this: Would you switch your money at a cost of over $52,000? The variable annuity investor would not have to worry about such a dilemma.

Performance

The track records of the best-performing variable annuities often exceed those of the top mutual funds, because the portfolio managers of variable annuities are overseeing a smaller pool of assets than their mutual fund counterparts. In fact, many variable annuities are managed by the same individuals and groups who oversee mutual funds. These "clone funds" have an enormous advantage over their larger brethren since they are smaller and can react to market conditions more quickly. More importantly, a smaller portfolio can be more selective in the securities it buys and sells.

Most mutual funds, due to their tremendous size, are forced to buy stocks and bonds that may not be their first or even hundredth choice. This is because the Securities Exchange Commission (SEC) requires a diversified mutual fund to follow certain rules of diversification. A variable annuity, on the other hand, can load up on the stocks and/or bonds it really wants. This is particularly true in the case of an initial public offering (IPO).

An IPO is a stock offered by a company that is going public for the first time. Often, a number of institutional buyers have been lining up trying to buy as much of the offering as possible. Unfortunately, there is only so much of the stock to go around. A billion-dollar mutual fund that is able to get $10 million of a hot new issue would be considered lucky. The same is true for an $80 million variable annuity account. If this $10 million worth of stock doubles in value, it will have very little effect on a billion-dollar mutual fund. However, for an $80 million variable annuity portfolio where $10 million represents 12.5% of total assets, it will have a very positive and dramatic effect.

All mutual funds keep a certain amount of assets in cash. These reserves are partly to satisfy investors' demands for partial or complete liquidations. Fund managers do not want to sell off securities in order to pay off shareholder requests. Annuities do not face this problem, since fixed and variable annuity withdrawals are much less frequent. Virtually the entire portfolio can be invested in stocks and/or bonds, making the accounts operate more efficiently and increasing long-term results.

"We've found that equity accounts within variable annuities have generally outperformed their mutual fund counterparts by about 1% to 3% annually," says Rick Carey, editor and publisher of the VARDS *Report* in Miami, Florida. The Variable Annuity Research and Data Service (VARDS) report calculates the performance of 85% of the existing variable contracts based on price appreciation and dividends minus contract expenses.

Carey cannot say exactly why annuity performance is so much better, although he believes insurers have done a good job of tapping some of the better equity managers. Stock portfolios under the annuity umbrella number less than 300, compared with more than 1,000 regular *equity* mutual funds. So insurance companies have been able to be a bit more selective about who runs their equity accounts.

Investors and financial commentators have been comparing the performance of individual stocks and bonds, as well as mutual funds and annuities, to various indexes and averages for over 100 years. However, there is a fault in such comparisons that is patently unfair to the security or portfolio being scrutinized. Such comparisons are not totally correct because of (1) transaction costs, (2) convenience features, and (3) management expenses.

None of the benchmark indexes or averages take into account transaction or commission costs. And no one can buy and sell a stock or bond without a cost. The typical cost for such a transaction ranges from 1 to 5% with 3% being an average. These fees are levied every time a buy or sell is conducted. Thus, the true total falls somewhere between 2 and 10% per complete trade (a buy and an eventual sell).

There are no convenience features or shareholder privileges to owners of individual stocks and bonds, but there is a roster of such features for the owners of mutual funds and variable annuities. These features include (1) the ability to switch within a family of funds at no or little cost, (2) toll-free telephone numbers to call for general and investment information, (3) regular reports, (4) an easy-to-follow tax form, also known as a 1099, provided each year (not used for annuities, since they grow and compound tax deferred), (5) systematic withdrawal plans for people who need monthly income, and (6) check-o-matic plans for investors who want to make contributions on a regular basis.

Most importantly, annuities and mutual funds provide professional management. The great majority of investors are not objective when it comes to making an investment decision. Do you sell when a position has dropped 5%, 25%, or 80%? How do you determine when you should buy? Do you add to a position when it has gone up 15% or dropped 34%? Buy decisions can be tough to make. Deciding when to sell, particularly when a portfolio is down, is often gut wrenching.

Fortunately, professional money managers can make these decisions for you. Not only can managers be completely objective, but they are armed with much more information. They are spending anywhere from 8 to 12 hours per day overseeing their mutual fund or annuity portfolio. There is no way you or I can match their training or time commitment. Doctors are not supposed to operate on members of their own family; it would be a similar mistake for you to make investment decisions about your own money. Maintaining objectivity is crucial in both circumstances.

When you add up the value of ongoing management, shareholder or contract owner features, and transaction costs, a much higher percentage of annuities and mutual funds outperform those indexes and averages they are often measured against.

Morningstar Study   During the first few months of 1992, Morningstar, a service which tracks the performance of mutual funds and variable annuities in a wide range of publications, conducted a series of studies based on performance and operating expense differences between mutual funds and variable annuities. Morningstar, considered the premiere source for fund analysis, wanted to see if variable annuities were "better" than mutual funds given certain levels of performance and costs.

The Morningstar report began with the following observation: "Variable annuities were originally created as an aggressive alternative to fixed annuities. Logically, it doesn't make much sense to switch from a fixed account to a variable annuity *money market* account—where yields are likely to be roughly the same, and expenses are likely to be higher. Likewise, as pension investments, variable annuities logically require an aggressive mien if they are to meet the potentially very hefty future retirement liability that they are intended to fund (it is estimated that the average 65-year old retiree can expect to live to age 85—requiring a substantial nest egg to maintain his or her pre-retirement standard of living)."

When you look at the operating expenses of variable annuities versus mutual funds, the typical mutual fund charges 1.25% annually for operating expenses while a similar variable annuity charges 0.77%, which means that variable annuities are 38% more efficient in this area. On the other hand, variable annuities charge an average 1.25% for mortality (the guaranteed death benefit), a practice that does not apply to mutual funds. Factoring in this extra expense, variable annuities are, on average, 0.77% more expensive to run each year than mutual funds.

Assume the following set of circumstances: (1) A variable annuity and mutual fund average a 15% annual return, (2) the investor is in a 37.4% tax bracket (state and federal combined), (3) there are no surrender charges for the annuity or mutual fund owner, (4) there is no penalty tax for the annuity owner, and (5) money is distributed from the annuity by annuitization or when the contract owner is in a 21.4% tax bracket. Given this situation, the variable annuity becomes a better investment after only two to three years. In fact, it takes only two years for a subaccount to begin to outpace a comparable mutual fund; the time horizon stretches out to five years if 5% rates of return are used.

Surprisingly, the Morningstar studies show that, based on actual performance of U.S. stock subaccounts (aggressive growth, growth, growth and income) and their mutual fund counterparts, the variable annuities still come out ahead after just five years, even assuming a 37.4% tax rate during accumulation (for the mutual fund owner) and 37.4% during the distribution period (for the annuity owner). In fact, even under the worst-case situation—high distribution taxes and a 10% IRS penalty—aggressive growth portfolios still beat aggressive growth mutual funds after nine years (the 10% penalty only applies to investors who are younger than 59.5 or are not disabled).

Looking at other categories, we see that annuities maintain their winning streak (again assuming a 37.4% accumulation tax rate for the mutual fund owner, a distribution rate of 21.4% for the annuity owner, and no surrender charges or IRS penalty). High-yield bond subaccounts and international stock subaccounts outperform their mutual fund brethren in less than four years (less than two years if we assume annual returns of 10%). Keeping these same assumptions, growth, growth and income, and balanced portfolios also come out ahead after just two years, assuming 12% returns all around. Even using just a 5% return, variable annuities become the winners within four years. Using actual performance figures of government and corporate bond subaccounts, variable annuities take the lead in just two years.

Variable annuities fare so well across the board because mortality costs are modest once you factor in the cheaper management and administrative expenses compared to "clone" mutual funds.

Withdrawal Options

Mutual funds allow you to make withdrawals or complete liquidations at any time. The same is true with annuities. But only annuities offer "lifetime options" in which the investor cannot outlive the income stream. Income options that you cannot outlive are discussed in a later chapter.

Investment Choices

When you invest in a mutual fund family, you have limited investment options and management styles to choose from. Several variable annuities offer you a choice of many different management styles within the same contract. However, in mutual funds, if you like the type of money managers found in Fidelity, Oppenheimer, American Funds, Nationwide, and Van Eck, you would have to invest your money with those five different mutual fund families. Yet there is a *single* variable annuity company, Nationwide Life Insurance, that offers you exactly the same managers who oversee these popular mutual funds. Exchanges within this variable annuity family can be made with one toll-free telephone call or even a letter—even though you are going from, say, Oppenheimer to Fidelity.

Safety

Mutual funds are prohibited from guaranteeing the rate of return or the safety of your principal. This is not true with annuities. In a fixed-rate annuity, you know exactly what your rate of return will be for each period, ranging from 1 to 10 years. The guaranteed period depends on the option you lock into. These same annuities also guarantee that your principal is secure every day; variable annuities offer the guaranteed death benefit.

No one has ever lost money in a fixed-rate annuity. No one has ever lost any principal in a variable annuity upon the death of the annuitant. However, the same cannot be said of mutual funds. Millions of people have lost billions of dollars in mutual funds.

Commonly Asked Questions

What protects against loss of my initial and/or ongoing investment?

Every variable annuity has inherent features that work to minimize risk and increase return, including the following:

Professional management. Like a family of mutual funds, all portfolios in a variable annuity are constructed and monitored by professional investment managers. Each portfolio has a stated objective, and the professional managers—backed by education, experience, and research—are better able to select the right investments to achieve the portfolio's objective.

Diversification. Even if you invest in a single portfolio, your risk is spread among many securities, reducing the possibility of losing a substantial amount due to any one security. Furthermore, you can invest in more than one portfolio.

Separate accounts. Variable annuity portfolios other than the fixed account option are part of a separate account, established and maintained apart from the company's general investment portfolio. The safety of your investment does not depend on the performance of the insurance company's own portfolio. Only the performance of the separate account portfolio you have chosen will affect your results.

Switching privileges. Most variable annuities permit you to reallocate your money among the portfolios, usually without charge as long as you do not move the money too often. Transfers among portfolios when interest rates or market conditions change can keep your earnings high.

Guaranteed death benefit. Variable annuities generally guarantee that in the event of death during the accumulation phase, your beneficiary will receive *the greater of* (1) the entire amount of your premiums, less withdrawals, or

(2) the current value of your investment. Some annuities provide more generous options.

Are annuities always a better choice than mutual funds?

No. Variable annuities are an alternative to mutual funds, just as fixed-rate annuities are an alternative to investing in a bank CD. It all depends on what you are trying to do with your money.

Why is there more information on mutual funds than annuities?

First, mutual funds are easier to understand. Popular publications emphasize the performance and features of mutual funds with much greater frequency. Second, the brokerage industry can make more money selling you mutual funds than annuities. Third, the insurance industry does not spend as much money promoting annuities as fund executives spend promoting mutual funds.

Are there as many fund managers to choose from if I invest in an annuity rather than a mutual fund?

There are not as many portfolio managers who fall under the annuity umbrella. However, you can usually find a fund manager with a solid track record who manages according to your investment objective. Also, as stated, annuity managers enjoy a better overall performance record than mutual fund managers.

How can I compare mutual fund results to annuity results on a regular basis?

Financial publications such as *The Wall Street Journal, Barron's,* and specialty services such as *VARDS* and *Morningstar* all provide fund and subaccount performance results you can use to compare and contrast specific fund and annuity accounts.

CHAPTER 10

How to Scrutinize an Insurance Company

How does the average person find out whether an insurance company can meet its commitments? How can an investor feel confident about an agent or broker that he or she is buying an annuity from? The quality of the insurance company is critical when selecting a fixed-rate annuity since investors' assets are commingled with those of the insurer. If the issuing company's portfolio becomes troubled, so do the contract owners'. Variable annuity monies are not mixed with the issuer's funds; therefore, variable annuity owners need not be concerned with the financial solvency of the parent company except perhaps for psychological reasons.

A trip to a reasonably stocked library or literature from a broker will provide you with the information you need to ensure that you are dealing with a strong insurance company. Additionally, you can ask questions of the financial planner, broker, or agent to determine whether he or she is a full-time, professional advisor or someone who is a part-timer or moonlighter. There are four areas you can look into: (1) the insurance company's rating, (2) claims-paying ability, (3) annual statements, and (4) investment portfolio.

Company Rating

Secure a copy of *Best's Agents Guide to Life Insurance Companies.* A. M. Best Company reviews the financial status of thousands of insurers and rates them on their financial strength and operating performance based on the norms of the life and health insurance industry. The Best Company has been in business since 1899. In 1906 it began rating life and health insurers. In 1934 Best stopped its alphabetical ratings (A+, A, etc.) and began a rating system based on general descriptions. In 1976 Best restarted its alphabetical rating. That system is in use today.

A. M. Best measures the performance of each company in the areas of competency of underwriting, control of expenses, adequacy of reserves, soundness of investments, and capital sufficiency. Best's current rating system has been in use for over 15 years. The ratings are as follows:

A+	Superior
A	Excellent
A−	Excellent
B+	Very good
B	Good
B−	Good
C+	Fairly good
C	Fair
C−	Fair

In the case of fixed-rate contracts, only deal with the top two or three categories. There are no advantages to dealing with a company that has a B+ or lower rating. In the case of variable annuities, the rating of the insurer is unimportant since your assets are not commingled with those of the company; lack of solvency or bankruptcy does not affect the value or integrity of variable annuity investments.

You might also survey the net yield on invested assets. Be suspicious of a company that is offering you a rate that is the same or higher than what they are earning on *your money*. Keep in mind that rapidly changing events can overtake the rating system before a new rating is published.

Claims-Paying Ability

Consumers often worry about an insurer's ability to make good on a policy or annuity. Again, turning to insurance company raters is the best way to investigate an insurer's soundness and claims-paying ability. There are two well-known rating systems: Moody's Investors Services Inc. and Standard and Poor's Corporation. Not all of the over 1,400 life insurance companies have been rated by these services, but a good number have.

Moody's rating system ranges from Aaa (highest quality) to C (lowest quality). Claims-paying ratings are Aaa, Aa1, Aa2, Aa3, A1, A2, Baa1, Baa2, Baa3, Ba1, Ba2, Ba3, B1, B3, Caa, Ca, and C. The numerical modifiers indicate whether a company is in the higher, middle, or lower end of the category.

Standard and Poor's ratings are similar, with categories ranging from AAA to BBB and speculative grade ratings from BB down to D. The D rating is for an insurance company placed under a court liquidation order.

Annual Statements

Annual statements are filed by each insurance company with every state the insurer does business in. Schedule F of this statement lists the amount of claims paid out and claims resisted. The lower the dollar amount paid out, the more financially sound the insurer is.

Investment Portfolio

Many fixed-rate annuity companies offer information on their investment portfolios in brochures and other marketing material. If you are interested in a particular company's investment portfolio, a phone call to the marketing department could prove beneficial. Other sources would be *The Wall Street Journal*, financial newsletters, and periodicals. When all else fails, contact your state's Department of Insurance.

An insurance company builds a sound business in part by diversifying its assets. It does this by holding a prudent mix of risk-free, low-risk, and, to a lesser degree, high-risk investments in its portfolio. If you are ready to buy an annuity, it is a good idea to ask for a summary of the insurance company's investment portfolio to determine how its assets are distributed. The money that you are about to place in the annuity (if the annuity has a fixed rate) will become part of those assets until it is time for you to withdraw the money. There is no right or wrong mix of investments, but there are industry norms that have proven sound.

The American Council of Life Insurance, a nationwide trade association of life insurance companies, reviews the annual financial statements of nearly every U.S. insurance company and reports that the industry portfolio averages are as follows: 15% government securities, 43% corporate bonds, 5% stocks, 22% mortgages, 3% real estate, 5% policy loans, and 7% in other asset categories.

The safest and surest securities are issued or backed by the U.S. government. These are universally considered to be risk free. Corporate bonds can be almost as safe, depending upon their rating. Corporate bonds are rated, or broadly categorized, as being either investment grade or junk. The industry norm for unsecured, non-investment-grade or so-called junk bonds is less than 6%.

Advisers say that consumers should stick to the roughly 20% of insurers reviewed by A. M. Best that get the maximum A+ rating—and particularly those that have had that rating consistently for years. A second rating from a company such as Standard & Poor's, Moody's, or Duff & Phelps provides an additional feeling of safety.

Looking at the investment portfolio, annual statements, claims-paying ability, and rating of the annuity issuer are important things for either you or your financial advisor to look into, but you may find that a summary of the insurance industry *as a whole* will answer most of your concerns. Therefore, the sections that follow include: an historical perspective on past life insurance insolvency's, an insurance industry study on the quality of investments owned by insurers, a response to the industry study by a trade group that represents insurance companies, and a description of what guaranty laws are, how they provide you with an extra layer of safety, what states offer such protection, and the dollar amount of coverage.

Past Insolvencies

During April, 1991, Executive Life Insurance Company was seized by California regulators due to defaults and declining values in its huge portfolio of junk bonds. Close to two thirds of the company's assets were invested in junk issues. Executive Life has 170,000 life insurance policies outstanding, with a face value of $38 billion. It sold 75,000 fixed-rate annuities with a value of $2.5 billion.

Prior to Executive Life's troubles, the best-known issuer of annuities that became insolvent was Baldwin-United, an annuity writer that failed in 1983. No investor lost any money due to Baldwin's demise, but contract owners learned in 1987 that they would get only a 7.5% return on their money, not the 13.6% initially promised.

Since 1974, 152 life companies have failed (half of those in the last five years). During the 1970s and early 1980s, an average of five companies went bankrupt annually. However, between 1983 and 1989, the annual average number of bankruptcies soared to 13. In 1989 alone, 37 life/health insurers went bust—the most ever in a single year.

In addition to these well-publicized failures, payments from guarantee associations to contract owners averaged $77 million over the last two years, a sharp increase from the $1.2 million paid in 1975. In 1989 the National Association of Insurance Commissioners (NAIC) targeted over 20% of all life insurance companies for immediate regulatory action. Five years ago, all of the life insurers rated by private agencies such as Standard & Poor's and Moody's Investors Services received the top grade. Now only 40% do.

A 1990 Study by the Life Insurance Industry

The U.S. life insurance industry, which boasts assets of well over $1 trillion, is heavily dependent on the annuity business. Investment income and annuity premiums account for nearly 60% of the total income of U.S. life companies.

At the same time, the ratio of capital to surplus has dropped, from 8% 20 years ago to 6.5%. Moreover, a number of companies have managed to inflate their surpluses artificially by manipulating policy reserves, using sales and lease-backs of offices and equipment to affiliated companies, entering into dubious reinsurance schemes, and employing level commission programs.

During 1990 and 1991, assessments by regulatory bodies to the life insurance industry to cover losses averaged $77 million annually, compared with the $1.2 million assessed during the recession year of 1975. The bulk of the assessments in the past have been for insolvencies of small group accident and health providers hurt by the inflation in medical costs.

The industry's junk exposure does not seem huge when compared to its invested assets. But remember that total industry capital is only 6.5% of assets. So the industry has nearly the equivalent of its entire net worth riding on an illiquid investment sector that was in a free fall for almost two years. Fortunately, 1991 and 1992 were excellent years for high-yield bonds.

Even more upsetting to some observers is the life industry's exposure to real estate. Mortgages and direct real estate investment comprise some 20% of total assets. Over 90% of the total consists of commercial mortgages on office buildings, hotels, shopping centers, industrial properties, and apartments.

Commercial mortgage delinquencies of life insurers, meanwhile, climbed from around 1% of all mortgages outstanding in 1980 to more than 4% in 1991. Moreover, this figure does not capture all distressed properties. Insurers typically do not report all their restructured loans, in which borrowers are granted concessions on interest rates, principal payments, or maturity schedules.

American Council of Life Insurance

In response to the 1990 industry study, the American Council of Life Insurance (ACLI) points out that even during a severe recession or depression, not all asset classes would collapse simultaneously. Junk bonds and commercial real estate might go down together, but that would be offset by a rally in the industry's holdings of high-grade bonds. Moreover, a large portion of the more established life insurers have "mature" blocks of real estate worth a great deal more than their book value. These holdings would prove to be a significant buffer against problems in the mortgage portfolio.

The ACLI also claims that a portion of life insurers' so-called junk bond holdings are in reality unrated, private-placement bonds. Frequently, these are sounder than many publicly traded, investment-grade issues because of superior loan covenants and collateral agreements that insurers are able to negotiate.

The state guaranty fund system could handle even multi-billion-dollar insolvencies without undue strain, because for most types of life insurance losses, payouts are spread out over many years as life or annuity benefits come due.

In response to increased public concern over the safety of the industry, The National Association of Insurance Commissioners

(NAIC) now requires insurers to increase and accelerate their special surplus reserves for junk bond holdings. Additionally, more states are adopting New York's regulation that limits junk bond holdings to less than 20% of a company's invested assets.

Guaranty Laws

If your insurer goes under, the effect on the value of your insurance policy or fixed-rate annuity hinges partly on where you live, what kind of policy you hold, and what the policy is worth. So far, regulators have made sure that the principal value of a policy or annuity contract has not been lost to policyholders.

A relatively low insolvency rate of five companies per year (1975–1982) has risen to an average of 16 per year with a high of 37 in 1989. Lifetime investments may become temporarily tied up (as in states where there are guarantee funds) or, worse yet, be permanently reduced or lost.

With $8 trillion of coverage in effect, the question of where the assets are invested becomes very important. Guaranty laws are a safety net. They set a limit of $100,000 on cash values of life insurance policies and up to $300,000 on combined benefits from all life insurance policies in force per person. Annuity investors are protected, and overall coverage limits normally are higher.

If you are a resident of one of the 46 states that have guaranty funds and conduct insurance or annuity business with a company licensed in your state, *you are protected.* However, guaranty laws are not in effect in Alaska, Colorado, New Jersey, Louisiana, and the District of Columbia. Insurance boards in each state decide whether or not to have a guarantee fund.

Table 10.1 lists the maximum protections allowed for each insured life. Maximum cash value usually applies to the cash value of life insurance policies. Where no figure appears for death benefits, the total cannot exceed the combined maximum protection. States indicated by a check mark also protect out-of-state residents when insurance companies headquartered within their borders go broke. Details vary and change often.

Guaranty laws protect annuity investors as well as the beneficiaries of life insurance. Coverage is for up to 80% of the annuity contract's value or $100,000, whichever is less; the same formula applies to the cash value in a life insurance policy. If you have

Table 10.1 *Maximum Protections Allowed for Each Insured Life, by State*

State	Maximum Cash Value	Maximum Death Benefit	Out-of-State Coverage
Alabama	$100,000	—	✔
Arizona	$100,000	—	✔
Arkansas	$100,000	—	
California	$100,000	$250,000	
Connecticut	$100,000	—	
Delaware	$100,000	—	
Florida	$100,000	—	
Georgia	$100,000	—	
Hawaii	$100,000	—	
Idaho	$100,000	—	
Illinois	$100,000	—	
Indiana	$100,000	—	
Iowa	$100,000	—	
Kansas	$100,000	$100,000	
Kentucky	$100,000	—	
Maine	$100,000	—	✔
Maryland	—	—	
Massachusetts	$100,000	—	
Michigan	$100,000	—	
Minnesota	$100,000	—	✔
Mississippi	$100,000	—	✔
Missouri	$100,000	—	
Montana	—	$300,000	
Nebraska	—	$300,000	
Nevada	$100,000	—	✔
New Hampshire	$100,000	—	✔
New Mexico	$100,000	—	✔
New York	—	—	
North Carolina	—	—	✔
North Dakota	$100,000	—	

(*continued*)

Table 10.1 *Maximum Protections Allowed for Each Insured Life, by State (cont.)*

State	Maximum Cash Value	Maximum Death Benefit	Out-of-State Coverage
Ohio	$100,000	—	
Oklahoma	$100,000	—	
Oregon	$100,000	—	✔
Pennsylvania	$100,000	—	✔
Rhode Island	$100,000	—	
South Carolina	—	—	✔
South Dakota	$100,000	—	
Tennessee	$100,000	—	
Texas	$100,000	—	
Utah	$100,000	—	
Vermont	—	$300,000	✔
Virginia	$100,000	—	✔
Washington	$500,000	—	✔
West Virginia	—	$300,000	✔
Wisconsin	—	—	✔
Wyoming	$100,000	—	

multiple policies, you automatically obtain multiple coverages. All annuities are covered by these guaranty laws, except for contracts *owned* by corporations or partnerships (or what is referred to in the insurance industry as "unallocated annuities").

In the case of an insurance company's death benefit, your protection against an insurer's insolvency is covered up to $250,000 per policy or 80% of the death benefit, whichever is less.

Do Your Homework

Smart insurance and fixed-rate annuity buyers do not rely on government watchdogs to safeguard their money. They do research and ask tough questions before investing or paying a nickel in premiums. Here are some points to discuss:

1. *How large the company is.* Only 6 of 48 companies that failed recently had assets of more than $50 million. Large companies, those with billions of dollars in assets and a national sales force, are better equipped to ride out financial cycles. Since they tend to sell many different products, downturns in one market segment are cushioned by gains in other segments. And since they pay higher salaries, big companies tend to attract the best management talent.

2. *The company's resident state.* According to an IDS (a division of Shearson, Lehman, Hutton) report, 70% of 130 insolvencies in the last 15 years occurred in nine states. The insurance commissioners of those states—Texas, Indiana, Oklahoma, New Mexico, Florida, Illinois, Arizona, Louisiana, and Washington—may not be tough enough.

   If an annuity company is regulated by a state such as New York, which is generally regarded as the most stringent state in the union, it is usually a safe bet. New York has the largest and most aggressive insurance department and some of the toughest regulatory standards.

3. *The company's major line of business.* Past insolvencies have involved mostly group accident and health insurers.

4. *Whether or not the company is heavily invested in junk bonds.* Life insurers own roughly $60 billion of the $200 billion in junk bonds outstanding. According to the IDS study, this equals 14% of the industry's total corporate bond investments and 6% of total assets. The American Council of Life Insurance reports that even a total meltdown of the junk market will have little impact on insurers because only a fraction of the industry's assets are invested in junk and because defaults on junk represent only one fifth of 1% of the industry's total assets.

5. *Whether or not the company appears on the NAIC's watch list.* The National Association of Insurance Commissioners (NAIC) tracks the financial performance of several thousand insurance companies. This data bank, known as the

Table 10.2 *Amount of Junk Bonds Owned by Large Insurers*

	% of Invested Assets Accounted for by Bonds Below Investment Grade	Junk as % of Total Surplus
Presidential Life	26.4	385
Jackson National	14.5	245
United Pacific	14.2	217
Kemper Investors	13.8	327
Southwestern Life	10.3	103
Sun Life of America	9.6	137
Guardian Ins. & Annuity	9.2	n/a

Insurance Regulatory Information System (IRIS), helps state regulators monitor the solvency of companies.

You could order an up-to-date IRIS report from the NAIC yourself. But it will be of little value. The NAIC does not release the names of companies whose financial status merits greater regulatory attention. It is best to contact your state regulator.

However, Joseph Belth, an insurance professor at Indiana University, has created his own "watch list" based on IRIS statistics. Companies with four or more unusual financial ratios end up on Belth's list. For a copy of Belth's watch list, send $10 to *Insurance Forum*, P.O. Box 245, Ellettsville, IN 47429.

Table 10.2 shows the amount of high-yield bonds, known as junk bonds, owned by seven of the largest insurers. Despite some of these dismal figures, the life insurance industry is in better financial shape than the thrift and banking industries. Although insurance companies lack the safety net of federal deposit insurance to protect policyholders, state guaranty funds allow the industry to "bury its dead" by indemnifying any losses suffered by policyholders of insolvent companies. In effect, state insurance departments either arrange for other carriers to take over troubled companies or pass the hat to make good the obligations of insolvent companies by assessing funds from other insurers doing business in the state. The assessments are proportionate to each company's share of its annuity or insurance business in the state(s) where the insolvency took place.

Commonly Asked Questions

Do state guaranty provisions really work?

The ability of a state to levy a special tax or draw from a pool of funds has not yet been put to the test on any kind of large scale. It appears that in the worst-case situation, investors would have to wait at least five years if a state's funds were insufficient and the troubled company was not bailed out by its peers. Again, this is something we have never seen. Troubled companies in the past have been anxiously taken over by other insurers.

How do these guarantees affect variable annuities?

Up to specified amounts, all annuities (fixed as well as variable) as well as life insurance policies are covered by these provisions. For practical purposes, such guarantees mean little to a variable annuity owner since his or her assets are not commingled with those of the issuer. The insurance company could go bankrupt during the year and the investor in that company's aggressive growth portfolio might experience a 45% gain that same year—and have immediate access to all previous and current earnings, growth and principal.

Are household name insurance companies safer than the others?

Not necessarily. You may be surprised to learn that some of the best-known companies, such as Kemper, Prudential, and Metropolitan Life, do not have the same safety as smaller, lesser-known annuity issuers.

If I stick with an insurance company highly rated by one of the rating agencies, I shouldn't have to worry about insolvency, should I?

Rating agencies are by no means perfect. In fact, they have been wracked with criticism over the past few years for being too lenient with insurance companies' balance sheets. Do all the research you can and weigh all the factors—positive and negative—of an insurance company. Do not go by a rating alone.

Why shouldn't I just invest in a variable annuity and leave all the insolvency worrying to fixed-rate and life insurance investors?

Remember, variable annuities are not without their own forms of risk. As an example, if you invest in a high-yield bond portfolio, some of the bonds could become worthless if the issuing corporation goes bankrupt. An aggressive stock portfolio could drop 10 to 25% in six months. And finally, even a portfolio of U.S. government bonds could drop in value if interest rates were to go up. True, with a fixed-rate annuity you do not take on any *investment* risk, but the annuity company could end up becoming financially troubled. However, the possibility of an insurer's going bankrupt relative to one of the securities markets' taking a dive is much slimmer.

CHAPTER 11

The Rating Game

Despite some recent insolvencies, there is general agreement that the life insurance industry as a whole is very healthy. Industry operating earnings have been increasing ever since the 1987 stock market crash. The most widely used rating service for insurance companies, A. M. Best, has testified before the U.S. Senate that company failures have been caused mostly by fraud, excessive growth, and mismanagement; only a small amount of the blame lies with investment losses. Indeed, the U.S. General Accounting Office has pointed out that there is no indication that large numbers of insurance companies appear to be in immediate danger.

These reassurances do little to quell the public perception that the insurance industry faces serious problems, particularly with regard to junk bond and mortgage holdings. In response to such concerns, the National Association of Insurance Commissioners (NAIC) has restructured its model for classifying bonds, holding companies to stricter rules. The companies themselves are changing their portfolios, and rating services are reevaluating their classification criteria. The industry is disseminating financial information to agencies and the public at a rate never seen before.

When reviewing the bond holdings of the insurance industry, bear in mind that less than 10% of all U.S. corporations now issue investment-grade securities. The remaining 90% must issue non-investment-grade or junk bonds. Despite such extreme figures, the industry's default rate remains at approximately one quarter of one percent.

In addition, many large insurers intend to cut back or cease purchasing commercial mortgages. These assets make up the largest holdings of all insurers, according to the Mortgage Bankers Association. But while large insurers have backed away from mortgages, close to half of the mid-sized insurance companies plan to invest in this type of security in the foreseeable future. It seems that large insurers are playing on public perception. Mid-sized companies have experienced delinquency rates of 1.9% among their real estate loans, compared to an industry average of 3.4%. The rating agencies used to be trusted to analyze and report this data to the public. But that has changed, too.

Faulting the Rating Services

The numerous bankruptcies of 1990 and 1991 have resulted in a loss of confidence in the rating agencies, particularly the best-known service, A. M. Best. The majority of the insurance companies that have suffered severe losses in recent years held an A+ rating from Best until just a short time before their problems became publicized. The lesser-known agencies, Standard and Poor's and Moody's, had also given high ratings to these same companies until the insolvencies began. What is the source of these misguided ratings?

All insurance rating agencies take their raw data from a company's annual statutory report, as designed by the NAIC (the report was changed in 1990). But even though rating services had information on Executive Life's (the largest insurance company default in history) large junk bond holdings, they should not be given all of the blame. Junk bonds became popular during the 1980s; there was not enough history or experience to forewarn the rating agencies about what might happen or the degree of decline. In fact, studies up to that time were generally positive about the issue of bond defaults and the resulting losses.

The majority of real estate losses have been due to unrealistic appraisals and large loan-to-value ratios. Such mistakes could have been prevented only if each mortgage had been analyzed carefully and all of the different appraisers been questioned thoroughly. This would have been an incredibly difficult and expensive task. Most rating agencies do review large mortgages but only closely scrutinize a sampling of the smaller loans.

Real estate industry losses have been caused by a simultaneous economic downturn and a quick decline in values after properties were developed. The succession of these events did not give the properties a chance to increase in value or build up some type of equity safety cushion. Fortunately, such a set of circumstances is very rare. Nevertheless, even these combined problems would not have hurt the insurance industry if there had not been massive policyholder withdrawals. This wiped out cash and marketable security reserves. In the past, rating services never factored a "run on the bank" into their ratings.

A. M. Best now analyzes the ability of an insurance company to withstand a "run." On a more positive historical note, over 90% of the insurance companies declared insolvent over the past decade did not have a Best rating within three years of their insolvency. Over the past dozen years, only six companies have been declared insolvent while holding a Best rating of B or higher.

Classifying the Rating Services

Agencies that rate or grade insurance companies are divided into two camps: those that charge the companies a fee to be rated and those that do not. *Weiss Reports* and *Standard and Poor's Insurer Solvency Review* do not charge fees. They make their money by selling their reports to investors and brokers.

The companies that charge a fee—Standard and Poor's (for reports other than the aforementioned), Duff and Phelps, Moody's, and A. M. Best—hope that insurers that do not have any kind of rating will look worse to agents and annuity purchasers than companies that have even a low rating. The rating system is designed so that weak insurance companies will try to improve their situation (to get more business).

A great number of insurers have either decided not to pay a rating fee or do not see the need to obtain a letter grade from more than one service. But those companies that obtain ratings have learned to use them as an advertising tool. More and more insurance companies with high marks are publicizing their rating(s) in newspapers, magazines, flyers, and letters to agents.

However, ratings can be very misleading. The average layperson cannot tell if a company's financials are bogged down by bad investments. Only someone who knows how to look beyond the letter grade would be able to see the true picture.

Evaluating a company's rating is a complex task. Even the rating companies themselves have a tough time with evaluations. Often, rating services do not agree. For example, *Weiss Reports* lists one insurance company as one of the five weakest, while A. M. Best reports it as "insufficient experience" and both Standard and Poor's and Duff and Phelps give the same insurer a AA− rating. To understand what goes into a rating and how the different raters approach this task, let us look at each of the major rating services.

A. M. Best Company

Starting in 1899, Alfred M. Best began what was known as an "independent watchdog" for the insurance industry. Today the company rates close to 3,700 insurance companies. A. M. Best has dozens of analysts and a support staff that numbers over 100.

Each insurance company's figures are updated and reviewed every quarter in the Best system. According to a company officer, Best is in "constant communication" with each of the insurance companies it reviews. The rating process begins by having the insurer complete a financial questionnaire at the beginning of each year. The questionnaire asks about the insurance company's profitability, leverage, and liquidity in comparison to insurance industry norms. Best feels that a company's numbers are the foundation for the evaluation. But interviews of the insurance company's officers tell the real story. When it comes to evaluating management, Best looks for competence, experience, and integrity.

In addition to a quantitative evaluation, Best also makes a *qualitative* judgment, looking at the quality of a company's investments. An insurer's assets are considered under the assumption that these items might have to be sold unexpectedly. In short, Best is looking for liquidity and quality. The greater the quality and the more marketable a security is, the less uncertainty there is about its future value. Mortgages, real estate, joint ventures, collateral loans, common stocks, and junk bonds are all reviewed based on their long-term prospects, not their short-term value.

After all of this is done, the insurer is assigned an analyst who rates the company on a letter scale ranging from A+ to C− (see Table 11.1, later in this chapter, for a description). Before the rating is assigned, however, several people have already compiled numbers and passed their information on to support analysts. These analysts then make a recommendation to a senior analyst. He or she either accepts or revises the recommended grade assignment before sending it to the rating committee. After the committee has discussed and reviewed the rating, the chief executive officer of the insurance company is contacted and asked for comment. The insurer then has the option of either accepting the rating or meeting with Best analysts and officers to discuss the letter grade.

Once this process is completed, Best publishes the ratings in their "Rating Monitor," a special section in its weekly publication, *Best's Insurance Management Reports*, followed by a write-up in the monthly magazine, *Best's Review* and the annual report, *Best's Insurance Reports*.

Many insurance companies are not rated for two reasons. First, the insurer may not want to pay the $500 fee. Second, the company may request that its rating not be published. In such a case, Best will still report on the company but will leave out the letter grade.

Standard & Poor's

Even though Standard & Poor's has been in the business of rating the financial strength and credit quality of debt issues (bonds and notes) for over 50 years, it has only been rating insurance companies for about 20 years. It has only been about 10 years since its ratings have been made public. Standard & Poor's reputation in the financial guarantee area has enabled it to assume a number-two position in a growing field of competitors.

At Standard & Poor's, the process of evaluating the ability of a life insurer to meet its obligations to policyholders begins with a formal letter. The letter commits the company to providing Standard & Poor's with the information necessary to achieve a final rating. All claims-paying ability ratings are voluntary, arrived at with the company's complete cooperation. A rating from Standard & Poor's costs anywhere from $15,000 to $28,000 per year, depending on the company's size.

Once the commitment has been formalized, Standard & Poor's assigns a lead analyst to work with the company. The analyst usually asks for the company's performance over the past six years, management and corporate strategy, industry risk, business review, operational analysis, capitalization, liquidity, and financial flexibility.

In addition to requesting records, financial statements, company press releases, and other documentation, the analyst sets up a meeting with the company's management team at the home office. The purpose of this meeting is to get a better picture of the quality of the company's management.

An essential part of the rating methodology is to identify the company's product lines and distribution systems and determine its strengths and weaknesses compared to the insurance industry as a whole. The following are among the questions asked:

What has been the compound growth rate of revenue over the last five or six years?

How is the revenue distributed by business unit, geography, product, and distribution channel?

What is the company's market share, both overall and for its individual product lines?

How are the company's investment assets allocated?

What is the interest rate risk of the company's interest-sensitive portfolios and guaranteed investment contracts?

What is the company's credit quality?

What is the company's asset concentration by industry and issuer?

What is the current portfolio yield?

What is the total return on the portfolio (including realized capital gains on equities)?

What is the average maturity and duration of the entire portfolio?

What are the delinquency ratios for select asset types such as commercial mortgages and below-investment-grade bonds?

The analyst then takes between two and three weeks to arrive at a preliminary rating of the company and submits the rating to a committee of his or her peers. The purpose of the committee meeting is to subject the preliminary rating to rigorous scrutiny, question its assumptions, verify the material facts, and challenge the analyst's conclusions.

By the end of the meeting, the committee must reach a consensus on what the final rating will be. That rating is then sent to the company for its approval. If the company approves the rating, Standard & Poor's deletes the confidential material and publishes it in three basic formats:

- *S&P's Insurance Book*. A loose-leaf collection of full, in-depth reports on each rated insurer, complete with charts and graphs. The book is updated throughout the year as necessary.
- *S&P Insurance Digest*. A quarterly publication containing the company's letter rating and a rationale for the rating.
- *S&P's Insurer Ratings List*. A monthly listing of insurers and their letter ratings.

If the company considers the rating to be incorrect, it can appeal the rating to the committee. If the company can prove that material information influencing the rating decision was inaccurate or misinterpreted, Standard & Poor's can change the rating accordingly. If the company cannot prove anything but disapproves of the rating, the rating stands. But the company then has the right to deny publication of the rating.

Moody's

Moody's Investors Service, which entered the bond-rating business in 1904, has been evaluating life insurance companies since the 1970s. In 1986 Moody's introduced insurance financial strength ratings to provide guaranteed investment contract (GIC) investors with objective, independent credit opinions. In April, 1991, the firm revised several elements of its benchmark capital ratio to reflect the changing nature of risk in the life insurance industry and to improve the accuracy and usefulness of the ratio.

Moody's offers financial strength ratings on nearly 80 life insurance companies, and the list continues to grow. The rated companies represent more than 60% of the life insurance industry's assets and more than 90% of total GIC assets.

Carriers pay about $25,000 for the service. Moody's sees its real clients as financial intermediaries such as brokers, pension plan sponsors, structured settlement advisors, and agents.

Much of Moody's attention has been given to carriers involved in the group pension and individual annuity business. Recently, coverage has expanded significantly from initial focus on companies selling GICs to annuity providers, universal life writers, and providers of other life products. Consequently, Moody's rates a number of small companies as well as the giant insurers.

Moody's Life Insurance Credit Report service includes a quarterly handbook, detailed reports on individual companies, "Special Comments" on industry issues, "Flash Reports" of rating actions, and access to analysts and briefings for investors.

For an annual fee of $125, Moody's quarterly *Life Insurance Handbook* gives ratings, explains its rationale, and provides executive summaries for all life insurance companies.

Carriers that contract with Moody's can refuse to have a rating published, but only if they do not become active in the market that Moody's currently covers (group pension and individual annuities). If the carrier enters the market or Moody's expands to cover their market, Moody's can release its rating.

Moody's ratings are opinions of the relative financial strength or weakness of insurance companies. They are intended to summarize the likelihood that an insurance company will meet its future obligations to policyholders. Consequently, in Moody's terminology, financial strength actually means "claims-paying ability."

In assigning a rating, Moody's uses much the same financial data that other rating companies use. Moody's is generally regarded as highly reliable on the issue of carrier solvency and keeps a sharp eye out for shifts in a company's financial health.

Applying its long-established system and expertise developed through the years as a bond and credit rating firm, Moody's takes pride in the objectivity of its analysis. However, the insurance unit includes only six senior analysts, an associate analyst, and a research associate for tracking the entire life and property-casualty insurance industries. That compares with a staff of over 100 at A. M. Best Co. Even so, Moody's analysts have broad experience; all have been active in the insurance business or related fields for at least seven years and spend 100% of their time conducting research and communicating with clients.

Duff & Phelps

The Duff & Phelps insurance company rating process, which costs an insurance company $17,000, was first used in 1986. It is divided into four parts.

First, Duff & Phelps requests company financial reports. After the reports have been received, representatives travel to the insurance company for an initial on-site interview. During that meeting, the rater meets in groups and individually with key management personnel, including the chief executive officer, chief financial officer, chief investment officer, and product managers.

Duff & Phelps next invites a group of executives from the insurance company to its Chicago headquarters to confer with members of the rating committee. This meeting gives the insurance company the opportunity to meet its evaluators and get a better sense of the rating process.

Finally, the rating committee—consisting of three to five financial and technical experts appointed by Duff & Phelps's management—convenes to establish a rating. It presents the grade and an analysis to the insurance company. The company can opt either to publish or discard the results.

The Duff & Phelps team emphasizes how the company answers questions and how it deals with each aspect of the rating process. For example, if in its investigation of a company Duff & Phelps learns that the company has invested heavily in cable television, evaluators ask company executives about their knowledge and whether or not they have sought expert advice. The rating team is looking for a solid philosophy.

For example, while new listings from Standard & Poor's and Moody's still placed Executive Life in the A range, Duff & Phelps had already downgraded the failing company to BBB upon assessing its managerial practices.

As part of its contract, the insurance company agrees to provide relevant financial information quarterly, for ratings updates. There is also an annual review meeting at the start of each new rating year. Duff & Phelps operates under the principle that company strength can change rapidly. If Duff & Phelps believes that a company has withheld information or has knowingly provided misinformation, that company can be dropped. This has never occurred.

Weiss Research, Inc.

Weiss believes a rating system should "flag potential problems in such a way that the average consumer will be adequately informed in a timely fashion."

Weiss employs about 50 people, including analysts, programmers, technicians, clerks, and customer service counselors. All but six of the firm's employees are located at its Florida headquarters.

Off-site employees, including writers and a consulting actuary, are located around the United States and maintain close contact with the main office through computer hookups.

Weiss developed a proprietary computer model that uses some 200 ratios derived from 750 pieces of data to determine an insurer's rating. Data for these calculations come from the statutory reports insurance companies submit to the state insurance commissioners, plus supplemental data from the companies.

Weiss does not interview managers of the insurance companies. "Good management will produce good results; and bad results cannot be explained away by discussions of management's experience," Weiss says.

The results of the analysis and the ratings are sent to companies with a request that the data be examined and verified. Some companies do not respond to these requests. Others object to the rating received. Still others object so strenuously that they threaten lawsuits.

Weiss Research receives quarterly reports from the insurance companies. New information is added to the analytical process and is reported in quarterly updates.

Table 11.1 (on pages 124 and 125) shows a summary of the different major rating services. The figures shown in parentheses represent the number of companies rated by the respective service in a given category.

Some Final Thoughts

Insurance companies are getting their money's worth when it comes to a favorable rating. Many of these issuers tout their grades in advertisements and even issue press releases to announce a stellar rating. Yet, in uneducated hands, ratings can be potentially misleading. Most sources agree that it is a mistake to rely too heavily on one rating service.

An annuity issuer does not need the top rating to be safe. Remember that ratings are still an opinion or interpretation; they are not a guarantee.

Commonly Asked Questions

Is one rating service better than another?

No. The A.M. Best Company is the best-known rating service and is certainly one of the best. Ideally, when you are shopping for annuities you should look for a top rating from at least two of the major rating services.

Why don't variable annuities stress their rating(s)?

The rating of an insurance company offering a variable annuity is not nearly as important as one that sells fixed-rate contracts. Unlike almost all fixed-rate contracts, variable annuity money is not commingled with the assets of the insurance company. Investors who participate in a variable contract need only worry about how the subaccounts are doing, not the financial solvency of the issuer.

On average, how often does an insurance company's rating change?

Very infrequently. The vast majority of companies that have a good rating will maintain their quality standing for years to come. You will occasionally read about a handful of companies being downgraded. This is not very common, particularly when you consider that there are well over 1,800 *life* insurance companies in the United States alone (close to 3,700 insurers if you include life, health, and medical).

How can insurance companies go insolvent if they are constantly tracked by rating agencies?

As stated, raters provide only an interpretation of a company, not a guarantee. Until recently, insurance company assets did not have to be marked to "market value." Thus, if an insurer bought a shopping mall for $80 million, that $80 million would be reflected on the

Table 11.1 Summary of Major Rating Services (Number of Companies Rated Shown in Parentheses)

Quality Level	A. M. Best	Standard & Poor's	Duff & Phelps	Moody's	Weiss
Superior	A+ (270)	AAA (69)	AAA (20)	Aaa (17)	A+ (6)
Excellent	A (237)	AA+ (38)	AA+ (8)	Aa1	A (25)
	A− (37)	AA (21)	AA (8)	Aa2	A− (25)
		AA− (24)	AA− (13)	Aa3 (34)	
Good	B+ (120)	A+	A+ (3)	A1	B+ (47)
		A (9)	A (6)	A2	B (108)
		A− (5)	A− (2)	A3 (22)	B− (69)
Adequate	B (70)	BBB+ (1)	BBB+	Baa1	C+ (103)
	B− (10)	BBB (4)	BBB	Baa2	C (335)
		BBB− (1)	BBB−	Baa3 (2)	C− (270)
Below Average	C+ (20)	BB+	BB+	Ba1	D+ (170)
		BB	BB	Ba2	D (136)
		BB−	BB−	Ba3 (2)	D− (29)

Financially Weak	C (10) C− (0)	B+ B B−	B+ (1) B B−	B1 B2 B3 (0)	E + (63) E (41) E − (5)
Nonviable		CCC CC (3) D	CCC CC D	Caa (1) Ca (0) C (0)	F (38)
Not Eligible for a Rating	(170)				U(268)
Significant Change in Management or Ownership	(27)				
Below Minimum Standards	(59)				
All Others	(349)				
Total	(1,379)	(175)	(61)	(78)	(1,738)

company's books as an asset; if the market price of that asset declined, it would still be shown as an $80 million asset. As the real estate market went bust, and many non-investment-grade bonds lost their value, insurers were stuck with illiquid assets. Rating agencies now look at the liquidity aspect of all investments.

If an insurance company is paying for its own rating, isn't it likely that it will get a good one?

No. If there were fewer insurance companies in the United States, a conflict of interest situation could arise. But the number of companies seeking ratings ensures (hopefully) that a clean and ethical process takes place. The symbiotic relationship between the rater and insurer should make investors feel comfortable that a rating is true, no matter how much the insurance company has paid for it.

CHAPTER 12

Group Plan Annuities: Do You Qualify?

School personnel, hospital employees, and members of nonprofit organizations are eligible to participate in a retirement plan referred to as a tax-sheltered annuity (TSA). These qualified programs are authorized under Section 403(b) of the Internal Revenue Code (IRC). Tax-sheltered annuities offer advantages not found in other types of annuities and retirement plans. If you are not a member of one of the groups described in the first sentence of this paragraph, skip the rest of this chapter and move directly to Chapter 13.

Tax-sheltered annuities are annuity contracts purchased from an insurance company. The participant can choose between a fixed and variable account. Contracts are issued either on an individual or a group basis. The insurer receives contributions directly from the employer. The participant's contributions may vary yearly. Contributions are spelled out in a salary reduction agreement—they are made from payroll deductions on a pretax basis. Despite the deductibility, social security taxes are withheld on the employee salary reduction amounts.

Tax-sheltered annuities and other types of 403(b) plans are intended for retirement. Under certain circumstances, money can be withdrawn without penalty before retirement. Such distributions are allowed dues to financial hardship, death, disability, or termination of employment.

Individual and Group Contracts

An individual contract means that each person participating in the retirement plan receives an actual contract. Under a group contract, each participant receives a certificate verifying participation and indicating that the contract is between the insurance company and the employer.

Individual contracts have certain guarantees that exist until the contract ends. Group plans have assurances that last for a certain period of time, such as five years. A major difference between individual and group contracts is flexibility. Individual contracts are portable. If you change jobs, there are several options to choose from: (1) Freeze the account; (2) transfer part or all of the account to a program offered by your new employer, assuming the new company has an existing TSA program; or (3) place part or all of the monies in an IRA. All of these options allow the account to continue to grow and compound tax deferred. If the changeover is made properly, no tax event will be triggered.

Movement of a TSA to another plan can escape IRS penalties and taxes but may not avoid withdrawal charges from the previous insurer. Generally, group contracts include some type of transfer fee. Individual contracts can normally be moved from one employer to another without charges.

Variable Funds

For an insurance company to offer variable policies, it must be registered with the Securities and Exchange Commission (SEC). A prospectus must also be given to the investor at, or prior to, the time of purchase.

Several variable contracts offer companion fixed-rate accounts. This allows the policyholder (investor) to transfer between the fixed and variable subaccounts with little or no cost.

Tax Benefits

The major attraction of TSAs is their income tax implications: (1) Contributions reduce your taxable income, dollar for dollar; (2) once invested, monies grow and compound tax deferred; and

(3) when withdrawals are made, you may be in a lower tax bracket, thereby minimizing the tax consequences.

The Accumulation Period

During the accumulation period, the employer is putting money in the TSA on behalf of the employee (participant). Contributions are made with before-tax dollars on a biweekly, semimonthly, or monthly basis. The monthly schedule is most commonly used. The insurer then deposits most or all of each contribution into the participant's account. How the money is actually invested depends on the options the participant elects.

When deposits are made on your behalf, a transaction charge may occur. Additionally, either quarterly or annually, a maintenance fee may be deducted from the account's balance. Some companies recover their expenses by charging a negligible amount during the accumulation period and a larger fee when monies are withdrawn.

The Payout Period

When you are ready to receive the distribution (payout) from the contract—usually at retirement—there are several options available. You can take it all out as a lump sum, make a partial withdrawal, roll over the account into an IRA or another TSA, or annuitize the contract and start receiving a series of monthly, quarterly, or annual payments.

If you choose to annuitize, the payment will depend on the rate offered by the insurer, the annuity option selected, and the amount being annuitized. Annuity rates are stated as the amount of monthly income that will be paid by the insurance company for each $1,000 accumulated. Some insurers allow the contract owner to select either a fixed or variable account during payout, regardless of the type of contract used during accumulation.

If a variable account is used during annuitization, no guarantees can be made regarding the monthly payment. If the portfolio does well, monthly benefits will increase and vice versa. For the insurer initially to select or later change the monthly benefit, it must select an assumed interest rate of return (AIR). For example, if the

AIR is 6% and the investment return to you each year is also 6%, the benefit will not change. If the return is 14%, the monthly benefit will increase. If the return is only 2%, the benefit will decrease.

Methods of Crediting Interest

The two most common methods used to determine the current interest rate to be credited to employee accounts are the *portfolio average* and the *banding* method. The portfolio average method reflects the insurer's earnings on its *entire* portfolio during the given year. All policy owners are credited with a single composite rate.

The banding approach uses a year-by-year means of crediting accounts. Employee contributions are banded together for that particular year. Each account is then credited with the yield the account earns. Thus, the contributed money for year X may earn 9%. But all of the previous years' contributions may, on average, be returning only 8%. The contributed money for year X would then, in this example, be receiving 9%, while the balance would be averaging 8%.

The banding method is advantageous to the investor when interest rates are rising. In a declining interest rate environment, the portfolio method is best.

Two-Tier Interest Crediting

Although the two-tier method is used, it is often misleading. The two-tier approach usually credits the contract with a lower rate of interest if a partial or total liquidation is made. It often has a substantial charge for withdrawals—a charge that may never disappear. Finally, accounts are credited an artificially low rate if a minimal payout or period is elected. These three aspects of two-tier policies allow a company to *appear* to pay competitive rates during the accumulation period. The rate is only realized if annuitization through the initial insurer is utilized. This locks the investor into one company for life.

As you can see, transferability (1035 exchanges) is discouraged because of the punishing rates *actually* received or credited. Comparing the current rate of return from a two-tier contract with rates offered from other types of contracts is misleading.

Two-tier policies are considered so unfair that they have been outlawed in certain states.

Current Trends in Crediting

Several companies no longer use a calendar-year approach in valuing the rate of interest to be credited to accounts. These companies now use a quarterly, monthly, or even daily method. The reasoning behind this more responsive method is to allow the insurers to be more competitive and also to move quickly to alter the credited rate if it is too high in relation to the actual yield on the company's portfolio.

A small number of insurers have adapted a provision called *market value adjustment*. This method adjusts the accumulated *fund balance*, not the yield, upward or downward. The adjustment is in the opposite direction of the movement in interest rates. If the current rate is higher for new contributions than other monies, the value of the investor's account will decrease. Conversely, a decrease in the *current rate* results in an increase in fund value. In this particular situation, accumulated monies can constantly change in value, even though you invested in a "fixed-rate" portfolio.

Variable Options

Variable TSAs are an alternative to the more conservative fixed-rate alternatives. These variable accounts offer the employee a range of options from money market funds to aggressive stock portfolios. The generic options available are discussed in detail in Chapter 6.

Contributions

The overwhelming majority of TSA contributions are made by the employee, as outlined in the salary reduction agreement. Contribution parameters are set by the insurer. Total annual contributions cannot exceed IRS limitations. The amount by which the employee's paycheck is reduced may be an exact dollar figure or a percentage of pay. The investments are normally sent to the annuity biweekly, semimonthly, or monthly.

However, another way to make a contribution is by transfer. The employee may move funds from one insurer to another or from one subaccount to another portfolio offered by the same insurance company. Transfers are made for one of the following reasons: (1) dissatisfaction with the current portfolio's performance, (2) changing employers, (3) a change in the employee's ability to take risk, (4) a change in the investor's retirement date, or (5) new employment with someone who does not offer TSAs.

IRS Publication 571 provides the guidelines by which an individual participant calculates his or her maximum exclusion allowance (MEA). Contributions in excess of 20% or exceeding $9,500 could result in audits. Additionally, in California most school districts have chosen to have the employee's retirement contributions contributed on a pretax basis, which will alter the calculation. Many insurance carriers offer software which provides the contribution limits.

Retirement Options

Upon retirement, you have a choice of several options: (1) Leave the money where it is and let it continue to grow until a later date, (2) withdraw part or all of the account, (3) take out the account balance in a series of payments over a period of years, (4) select a fixed-rate or variable contract and annuitize, (5) transfer the balance to another insurer, or (6) move the account to an IRA rollover that is invested in another annuity or a mutual fund family.

Some participants will accumulate funds with one company and then elect to transfer the entire account to another insurer that offers a better annuitization schedule. If you consider such a move, make certain you are familiar with any withdrawal costs or lost opportunities.

If a participant decides to annuitize, the type of plan chosen should depend on the person's health, dependents, and longevity. If the employee is in poor health, a straight life annuity is probably a poor choice. A life annuity with period certain or a joint and last survivor option would almost certainly be a better choice. If you have dependents that will continue to need financial support after your death, the period certain or joint and last survivor option would again be a wise choice. Without dependents, a life annuity would provide the highest periodic payouts. Finally, a retiree who does not want to outlive his or her income should look at one of the life options instead of just considering a lump sum or installment payment.

A creative retirement approach would be to use an AIR, which is found only with variable annuities. All variable accounts require an AIR as the basis for initial and subsequent payments. Many variable annuities allow the participant to select his or her own AIR in calculating the initial payment level. The higher the AIR used, the higher the *initial* checks will be. Other companies offer only one AIR.

Since annuitization under a variable contract can be risky, most companies offer a fixed-rate account. Fixed-rate portfolios do not have AIR to consider; the *insurance company* determines its current annuitization rates. These rates, in turn, determine the amount of your monthly benefit. Fixed contracts normally provide a minimum rate. It is highly unlikely that the offered rate will ever be this low. Thus, when comparing fixed-rate annuitization programs, use the *current* annuity rates.

Qualified annuities are used in paying out retirement income from pension plans, profit-sharing plans, 401(k)s, IRAs, and 403(b)s. Because the dollars that purchase the annuity are qualified, the annuity income generally is considered fully taxable as it is received. If the employee or his or her heirs decides to annuitize the qualified annuity retirement plan, there may be an up-front, one-time premium tax. In California, the state premium tax is 0.50%. This rate is substantially lower than the 2.37% California charges when a non-qualified contract is annuitized.

Loans

A number of insurers allow you to borrow a portion of your TSA. However, there are several reasons why a company may not allow loans. The chief reason is probably the IRS, which restricts the amount and period of any loan. The Internal Revenue Code (IRC) states the following:

1. A loan is taxable if it exceeds 100% of the employee's account or $10,000, whichever is less, *if* the account is less than or equal to $10,000.
2. A $10,000, or greater, loan is taxed if the participant's account is more than $10,000 but less than $20,000.

3. If the value of the account is over $20,000, a loan is also taxable if the amount borrowed is 50% of the value of the account or $50,000, whichever is less. The $50,000 amount referred to here is reduced by any net loan repayments made by the employee during the preceding 12 months.

4. Loans (except certain real estate related loans) must be repaid within five years.

5. If the loan is not repaid in time, any outstanding amount is immediately subject to taxation. It could also be subject to a 10% penalty tax.

6. If a loan is in default, the insurance company involved is required to notify the IRS and the participant.

7. If the loan ever exceeds the value of the employee's account, any excess is taxed.

In addition to these IRS restrictions, a number of companies have a loan minimum and require that a certain amount remain in the investment after the loan is made.

Those insurers which offer loans may also levy a fee when the loan is taken. These charges may be in the form of an initiation fee, administration fee, or account maintenance fee. Additionally, there is a special provision in the TSA contract allowing insurance companies to charge interest on the amount of the outstanding loan. The loan rate may be a flat fee or tied to some well-known index rate. Most companies also prohibit a second loan until the first is fully repaid.

Loan Protection

Due to the potential adverse tax and penalty consequences of TSA loans, prospective borrowers should contact their annuity company and find out about possible safeguards. These protective measures can protect against a late payment, also referred to as a *technical default*. Some insurers state that any payment due, but unpaid, may be deducted from the remaining funds in an account. This type of "forced payment" may be considered a withdrawal. But any withdrawal charges would be minor in comparison to a loan default.

Death Benefits

Most insurance companies do not charge any type of fee or penalty for a liquidation due to the death of the participant. If a penalty is levied, it could be the reduction of interest via a lower-tier withdrawal rate. You may wish to review the preceding discussion of two-tier interest crediting.

Upon the death of the employee, most companies will pay out the total account value. The death benefit may be taken as a lump sum, or the contract can be annuitized by the beneficiary. A few insurers offer additional payment options. Processing time for death claims, once all required paperwork has been received (e.g., certified copy of the death certificate) averages about two weeks. Sometimes the process may take only a few days.

TSA Expenses

Every TSA has expenses. But some of them are more identifiable than others. There are two basic approaches used by insurers in obtaining these fees: explicit and implicit. *Explicit* charges are clearly spelled out and visible. They may be applied regularly throughout the year, such as when the account is valued, when a contribution is received, when a loan is made, or when a withdrawal occurs.

Implicit charges are made indirectly and can often be much higher than their explicit counterparts. An implicit "charge" might be the difference between the returns the insurer actually earns versus the amount credited to your account. Another hidden cost may take place if, and when, the contract is annuitized. That cost will include a profit margin (the spread between what you receive and what the account actually earns) and expense charges. It is not unusual for a participant to ignore or underestimate the number and magnitude of implicit charges.

Insurers have the right to alter or amend TSA contracts. This privilege is usually quite broad. Such alteration can affect the amount of any charges made, interest credited to the account in the future, annuity rates per $1,000 annuitized, and other provisions described in the contract. For the most part, only group contracts can be altered without your permission. Individual TSAs can be changed only with the permission of the investor.

Commonly Asked Questions

Are TSAs different from annuities?

No. A tax-sheltered annuity (TSA) is a *type* of annuity that is offered to certain employees. However, unlike other annuities (which are funded with *after*-tax dollars), TSAs are contributed to with before-tax dollars (the contributions are deductible). The performance of a TSA depends on whether or not a fixed-rate and/or variable account is offered as well as current market conditions and the outlook for interest rates.

What do I do if I am eligible for a TSA but haven't used one before?

First, contact your employee benefits coordinator or one of the companies offering the annuity and find out if you can participate in a "catch up" (this means that you can add additional monies over the next several years to make up for what you missed out in the past). Second, find out how much you can contribute during each pay period, whether or not there is a catch-up provision. Third, find out what investment options are available to you. Fourth, contact your financial advisor and go over the different choices in light of your other holdings, risk level, goals, and time until retirement.

Can I contribute to both a TSA and a "regular" annuity?

Yes. Depending on your needs, however, it may be wiser to beef up your TSA contributions. That way, expenses and fees are kept to a minimum. But if your circumstances warrant a double investment, there is no law against you investing in both.

Why are rates of return so different with TSA accounts?

Because TSAs are a group annuity. The different expense and rate of return calculations are far more complex because of the number of plan participants involved.

What if I don't agree with a change in policy of my group contract?

You can opt out. That is one of the downfalls of a TSA; the individual is subject to the decisions of a group as a whole. Usually the changes to any TSA account are done with maximum input from participants. So you do have a say. Whether the final decision meshes with your financial plan is another issue.

CHAPTER 13

Structuring Annuities into Your Financial Plan

There is no single "best" investment. Indeed, every legitimate investment is appropriate for some investors during certain periods of their lives. For example, a money market account or bank CD might be a proper choice for an aggressive investor who needs a temporary place to park his or her money before making an investment decision. At the other extreme, a mutual fund that specializes in international stocks might be a good choice for a conservative investor who needs a hedge against inflation and wants to decrease the risk of holding just U.S. stocks.

If there was a "best" investment, there would be no need for stockbrokers, financial planners, or investment counselors; you and I would simply place all of our money in one place. Unfortunately, the world of investing is not that simple. In fact, it can be quite complex. This chapter will give you some general and specific ideas about how your entire portfolio can be structured. In addition, you will learn how to determine if fixed-rate and/or variable annuities should be one or more of your investments. Let us begin by trying to determine what you are trying to do with your money.

Growth or Income?

Everyone is trying to do something with their money. Some people need current income, while others are looking only for growth. Still others need some current income but also need some growth to offset the effects of inflation. Thus, the first step is to determine if you need (1) growth (appreciation), (2) current income (checks sent to you on a regular basis), or (3) some growth and some income (you need to get just a little more money each month to augment your other sources of income).

Risk Level

After you have determined your needs, a risk assessment is in order. Most people have a good idea of how much risk they can accept. As a broad generalization, you are either conservative, moderate, or aggressive. To help you determine your risk profile more precisely, look at Figure 13.1 and choose the single description that best describes you.

While reviewing the expected range of returns and the probability of losing up to 5% of your money in any given year, keep in mind the following points: (1) The loss would not be permanent, (2) the recovery time needed to make up the loss could be as little as three months or as long as three years, and (3) returns become more predictable if the expected holding period is five years or longer. This is why a time frame must be factored into any financial plan.

Investor Profile	Expected Range of Returns Annually	Odds of Losing 5% of Your Money
Very Conservative	5–8%	Zero
Conservative	7–10%	1 in 25
Conservative to Moderate	9–12%	1 in 15
Moderate	11–14%	1 in 9
Moderately Aggressive	14–17%	1 in 7
Aggressive	16–19%	1 in 5

FIGURE 13.1 **Investor Profiles.**

Time Horizon

Barring an emergency, you are the only one who knows when you will need money and how much. Some investments are designed to be held for the short term (0 to 3 years), others work best if they are owned for an intermediate period (4 to 7 years), while a few vehicles perform best if they are owned for a long time (8 to 14 years). *Short-term investments* include bank CDs, money market funds, short-term global income funds, and bonds that are going to mature in just a few years. *Intermediate-term investments* include tax-free or taxable bonds that mature in less than a decade, mutual funds or variable annuities that are "balanced" or "total return" (a portfolio of stocks and bonds), growth and income stocks, foreign securities, growth stocks, and high-yield bonds. A *long-term portfolio* would include municipal bonds, government securities, variable annuities, and/or mutual funds that invest in aggressive growth, growth, international stocks, and growth and income securities as well as all-cash (nonleveraged) leasing programs, cable television deals, and REITs (real estate investment trusts).

Equities, or stocks, perform the best of any asset class over time. So the longer your holding period, the more likely you are to do well. Not only are the returns going to be more predictable, but the chances of a loss are greatly reduced. For example, considering the past half century, the chances of making money in the stock market during any given calendar year are 70%. If the time horizon is extended to three or five years, the chances of making money are 95%. Over any 10 consecutive years, the odds of showing a gain are 100%. These percentage figures become even more attractive if you are invested in a variable annuity or mutual fund that has the benefit of professional management.

Like other things in life, a specific risk level and time horizon may not be exact or may not apply to all of your holdings. Thus, a blended approach may be needed.

Blending Investments

Like most people, you may find that you do not want all of your investments to be conservative, moderate, or aggressive. You may also discover that the majority of your assets can be invested for one time period but that some can be left in for a different period of time.

There is nothing wrong with this; in fact, this approach is common. Often, a conservative investor wants to be a little risky with 5 or 10% of his or her portfolio. Conversely, a moderately aggressive person may need to know that $15,000 will always be available as a cushion or emergency fund.

These nuances or special considerations can be worked out with your financial advisor. You may want to use an investment pyramid, allocating the largest portion of your portfolio to less risky investments and working with smaller amounts as the risk increases. But before going to an investment counselor, take a few minutes and determine your tax bracket. It is always best to have a game plan of your own before seeing an advisor. Specifically, you need to find out how much income must be sheltered in tax-free bonds, annuities, and/or leasing programs. An overriding concern should always be what you make after factoring in the effects of income taxes.

Tax Tables: It's What You Keep That Counts

Table 13.1 combines federal and state income taxes. This table, which features California state income taxes, shows the full impact of taxes: how much is going to your state and federal governments. The state you live in may have higher or lower taxes than California. If you do not know your state tax bracket, the table will provide you with a good approximation.

Once you have determined your state tax bracket, take this figure and multiply it by your federal tax bracket. The resulting figure is what you should subtract after having added your state and federal brackets together. This is because you can deduct state income taxes from your federal return. For example, if your state bracket is 8% and your federal bracket is 28%, your combined bracket would be calculated as follows: $(28\% + 8\%) - (8\% \times 28\%)$ = your effective or combined tax bracket ($36\% - 2.24\% = 33.76$, your real tax bracket).

When calculating your taxable income, make sure that you exclude (1) any earnings or growth in a retirement plan, such as an IRA, Keogh, or pension plan, that has not yet been distributed to you; (2) interest from all tax-free bonds; and (3) growth and/or interest in your annuity that you have not yet withdrawn.

Table 13.1   *California State and Federal Income Tax Tables Combined*

Taxable Income: Single	Taxable Income: Married	State and Federal Bracket
0–$4,400	0–$8,800	15.85%
$4,400–$10,400	$8,800–$20,800	16.70%
$10,400–$16,400	$20,800–$32,900	18.40%
$16,400–$22,800	$32,900–$45,600	20.10% up to $20,400, then 33.80% (if single); 20.10% up to $34,000, then 33.80% (if married)
$22,800–$28,800	$45,600–$57,700	33.80%
$28,800–$100,000	$57,700–$200,000	34.70% to 37.40%
$100,000–$200,000	$200,000–$400,000	37.90%
$200,000 and over	$400,000 and over	38.60%

How Much Should You Invest in Annuities?

Once you have determined risk, time, tax bracket, and financial needs, you must consider how much of your portfolio should be invested in either fixed or variable annuities. There is no one easy answer. After all, we are dealing with investments that not only provide tremendous tax benefits; they can also be structured for current income and/or future growth. Depending on what financial goals you want to accomplish, annuities can be a very large or a very small portion of your portfolio.

By now you should have learned or determined (1) all of the advantages and disadvantages of annuities, (2) what you are trying to do with your money, (3) your risk level, (4) your time horizon, and (5) your tax bracket. These factors will determine how much of a role annuities will play in your financial and estate plan.

Annuities are the ideal choice for someone who is in a moderate or high tax bracket and is looking for a way to shelter current income or growth over a long period of time. Fixed-rate annuities might be a smart alternative for CDs, money market accounts,

GNMAs, Treasury Bills, or other government obligations, particularly if you are the type of investor who would only need to touch such monies in the case of unforeseen circumstances. Variable annuities might be a proper choice for a taxpayer who is in a moderate or high tax bracket and is tired of paying taxes on capital gains and dividends and interest from securities. They would also be a good substitution for mutual funds that exhibited high turnover rates (the frequent trading of stocks or bonds).

Someone who is looking for long-term growth and is in a federal tax bracket greater than 15% should consider investing in annuities as part of his or her overall portfolio. Those investors who want current income should not be put off, either. Fixed-rate and variable annuities can be structured for current income. Checks can be mailed automatically on a monthly, quarterly, semiannual, or annual basis. Income can be distributed for a set period of time or for the duration of your life expectancy (and/or that of your spouse, friend, child, etc.). You decide on the frequency and duration of the distributions. And, as you learned previously, a substantial portion of these checks can be tax advantaged for several years.

You have a great deal of latitude in deciding what percentage of your total portfolio should be in annuities. The following sample portfolios will help you get a better idea of how to apportion your portfolio.

Sample Portfolios

Very Conservative (Average Annual Return of 5 to 8%)

20% one-year fixed-rate annuities

15% fixed-rate annuities with a three- to five-year guaranteed (locked-in) rate

10% variable annuities: 70% in U.S. stocks and 30% in foreign stocks

15% short-term global income fund (an interest-bearing type of mutual fund)

20% money market funds (for everyday use or in case of an emergency)

20% municipal or U.S. government bonds that mature in 10 to 20 years

Conservative (Average Annual Return of 7 to 10%)

15% fixed-rate annuities with a three- to five-year guaranteed (locked-in) rate

20% variable annuities: 60% in U.S. stocks and 40% in foreign stocks

25% short-term global income fund

10% money market funds (for everyday use or in case of an emergency)

20% municipal or U.S. government bonds that mature in 10 to 20 years

10% nonleveraged leasing program or REIT (real estate investment trust)

Conservative to Moderate (Average Annual Return of 9 to 12%)

15% variable annuity subaccount or mutual fund: growth stocks

15% variable annuity subaccount or mutual fund: foreign stocks

20% short-term global income fund

10% money market funds (for everyday use or in case of an emergency)

10% municipal or U.S. government bonds that mature in 10 to 20 years

15% all-cash (nonleveraged) leasing program and/or REIT

15% global bond fund or variable annuity that invests in global bonds

Moderate (Average Annual Return of 11 to 14%)

10% variable annuity subaccount or mutual fund: growth stocks

20% variable annuity subaccount or mutual fund: foreign stocks

10% variable annuity subaccount: growth and income portfolio

15% short-term global income fund

5% money market funds (for everyday use or in case of an emergency)

15% all-cash leasing program and/or REIT

15% global bond fund or variable annuity that invests in global bonds

10% variable annuity subaccount: aggressive growth or small capital growth

Moderately Aggressive (Average Annual Return of 14 to 17%)

10% variable annuity subaccount or mutual fund: growth stocks

25% variable annuity subaccount or mutual fund: foreign stocks

10% variable annuity subaccount: growth and income portfolio

15% short-term global income fund

10% all-cash leasing program and/or REIT

10% global bond fund or variable annuity that invests in global bonds

20% variable annuity subaccount: aggressive growth or small capital growth

Aggressive (Average Annual Return of 16 to 19%)

25% variable annuity subaccount or mutual fund: growth stocks

35% variable annuity subaccount or mutual fund: foreign stocks

15% variable annuity subaccount: growth and income portfolio

25% variable annuity subaccount: aggressive growth or small capital growth

Like other investments, before you invest in any annuity, consult your investment advisor. He or she should be able to provide you with additional information and possibly recommend specific companies that are not listed in this book. Remember, as you or your advisor consider different contracts, look for companies that have been in existence for several years, enjoy a strong reputation in the financial services community, and include the subaccounts and provisions that are important to you.

Commonly Asked Questions

What if my financial plan or goals change?

A good financial plan should always be flexible enough to take into account different scenarios. Annuities, as investments, can be structured or restructured to fit into different plans. Thus, it is important to set up financial goals and keep in touch with your advisor as your needs change.

How often should I move my assets around?

Often, investors see tables that list the 10 best mutual funds or variable annuities and rush out to invest in these portfolios. Do not attempt to "chase last year's winners." What performed well last year may do poorly this year. A good example is real estate. It was a great investment during most of the 1980s, and now no one seems to like it. Aggressive growth stocks were hot in 1991, but they were unpopular during most of the previous decade. The list goes on and on. It is often better to stick with the original investments allocated in your financial plan unless your needs change.

Is it important to invest in several different categories of annuities?

Because no one knows what the next best-performing investment category will be, diversification is key to a healthy portfolio and investment plan. Smart investors know that they cannot predict the future, and therefore they spread out their money among several different categories. Such a strategy reduces risk and often increases your return.

What does it cost to have a financial plan drafted?

A comprehensive plan can cost anywhere from several hundred to a few thousand dollars. Before you pay for a financial plan, interview the planner and find out what you are getting for your money. Find out the advisor's background and ask for referrals.

CHAPTER 14

The 10 Best Fixed-Rate Annuities

There are several hundred different fixed-rate annuities. This chapter looks at 10 of the best. The selection process was based largely on a November, 1991 study by *Best's Review*. In its study, Best used the leading fixed-rate annuity offered by each of approximately 100 different issuers. The study covers the period from July 1, 1986 through June 30, 1991. The policy values shown are net of any stated expense charges. Both the accumulation and surrender values are shown on a cumulative basis. *Surrender value* refers to what a contract owner would receive if he or she were to take money out, in excess of the free withdrawal privilege, during each of the five years shown.

Most of the rates shown in the Best study were guaranteed for one year; some of the contracts had longer guarantee periods. This is an important point because it shows the integrity and/or money management skills of the annuity issuer. Some companies offer high initial rates to attract investor dollars, but then they lower the rate during subsequent periods knowing that the penalty will make it less likely for the contract owner to move his or her money to another insurer.

This listing of companies is from best to worst. That is, the contract with the highest surrender value at the end of the fifth year is the first fixed-rate annuity shown, and so on. In several cases, the accumulation value (what has been credited to the client's account) will be higher, and better, than some of the contracts shown as being "better." There is really no "worst," since all of the companies shown were the top performers in the study. For comparison purposes, the average $10,000 fixed-rate annuity had an accumulation value of $14,740 at the end of five years and a $14,270 surrender value at the end of the same period.

The format is designed to show you those features of a contract that you should consider closely, including historical figures and general information about the offering company. By including the telephone number and address, you can easily contact these companies for literature either directly or through your investment advisor or broker.

Each fixed-rate annuity highlighted includes the following information: how much is accumulated at the end of each year, the surrender value (which takes into account any remaining penalty), the rating, investment options, bail-out provisions, free annual withdrawals, the minimum guaranteed rate, and a company profile.

The *accumulation value* is the amount you have accumulated in your policy to date.

The *surrender value* is how much the policy would be worth, less surrender charges and penalties, if you were to cash it out today.

The *rating* shown indicates the financial safety of the insurer as measured by one or more independent rating services.

Investment options show the different contracts offered to policyholders. Most of the companies listed in this chapter only offered a one-year guaranteed rate of return.

The *bail-out provision* protects investors if the insurer offers a poor renewal rate. That is, the annuity contract may have a six-year penalty clause and an attractive one-year locked-in rate of return. After the first year, the renewal rate may not be competitive, however. In this case, the contract owner must either accept the new yield or be faced with a possible surrender charge, unless the bail-out provision can be used.

Free annual withdrawals show how much of the investment can be taken out each year. Most companies allow the investor to take out 10% per year. Some insurers allow 10% of the contract's then-current value, and others allow 10% of the original investment. Still other companies restrict the free redemption to periods after the first contract year. A few companies allow investors to take out as much money as they wish at any time, without incurring a penalty from the issuer.

The *minimum guarantee rate* refers to the assured rate of return, no matter how low interest rates fall. This rate, usually 4%, was of no interest to investors in past years but is now gaining notice since bank CD rates have fallen.

In addition to the aforementioned items, each fixed-rate annuity listed here includes a company profile, performance figures, and a commentary. The *company profile* is intended to give you a thumbnail sketch of how long the insurer has been in business, an approximation of the company's size, and how its assets are invested. *Performance figures* show how a typical $10,000 contract performed during each of the past five years ending 1991. The *commentary* section will give you an idea of the company's consistency, or its ability to offer as high a yield as possible over the past five years. The surrender charge, also referred to as the penalty schedule, is also detailed.

Benchmark

United Pacific Life
3301 9th Avenue South
Federal Way, WA 98003
1/800-428-8511

Rating	A (Best), BBB (S&P), Ba1 (Moody's)
Investment options	1-, 2-, and 4-year guarantee periods
Bail-out provisions	Free, if rate drops by 1%
Free annual withdrawals	10% per calendar year
Minimum guaranteed rate	4%

Company Profile

United Pacific Life began operations over 30 years ago. Today its assets are in excess of $5.5 billion. Approximately 90% of its assets are in bonds, and less than 16% of its holdings are in high-yield bonds. Less than 3% of its holdings are in real estate; the firm owns no mortgages.

As of the middle of 1992, the company's 10 largest industry holdings were as follows:

29% utilities	6% consumer products
14% oil and gas	5% capital goods (diversified)
9% forest and paper	4% government obligations
8% banks and real estate	4% telecommunications
7% chemicals	3% media and cable

Performance

Year	Accumulation Value	Surrender Value
1	$10,940	$10,480
2	$11,950	$11,440
3	$13,010	$12,470
4	$14,150	$13,350
5	$15,380	$15,350

Commentary

At the end of five years, an initial $10,000 grew to $15,380. In 1986, the company's rate was 9.05%; it then dropped to 8.50% a year later and stayed level until the end of the 1991 study.

Benchmark has a seven-year penalty period. The penalty starts off at 7% during the first year and declines by 1% each subsequent year. Withdrawals in excess of 10% per calendar year during the first seven years are subject to this schedule.

Future One

Ameritas
P.O. Box 82550

Lincoln, NB 68501
1/800-745-9995

Rating	A+ (Best), AA (S&P), A (Weiss)
Investment options	1 year
Bail-out provisions	None
Free annual withdrawals	10% per calendar year after one year
Minimum guaranteed rate	4.5%

Company Profile

Six years ago, the name of this firm was changed from Bankers Life of Nebraska to Ameritas. The company has been in existence for 105 years and has assets in excess of $1.5 billion. Its portfolio is mostly comprised of bonds with a wide range of maturities. Less than 2% of its assets are in high-yield bonds.

Performance

Year	Accumulation Value	Surrender Value
1	$10,360	$10,910
2	$11,560	$12,040
3	$12,750	$13,150
4	$14,010	$14,300
5	$15,280	$15,510

Commentary

At the end of five years, an initial $10,000 grew to $15,280. In 1986, the company's rate was 8.40%; it then climbed to 10.60% in 1987 and settled down to 8.70% by the end of the study in 1991.

Ameritas has a seven-year penalty schedule. Withdrawals made during the first three years are subject to a 6% penalty; thereafter, the penalty decreases by 1% for each of the next four years. Redemptions made after the seventh year are not subject to any company penalty.

Once the guaranteed interest rate has ended, contract owners receive a renewal rate that is based on a "banded method." (The first $5,000 receives one rate, the next $20,000 receives a slightly higher rate, and the next $25,000 receives an even higher yield.)

Some companies offer investors a comparatively high rate of return to begin with and then lower the rate after the initial guarantee period has ended, but the penalty period still exists. Ameritas uses a method that is inclined to keep existing contract owners happy. Historically, its renewal rates have been at least one half percentage point higher than what it usually offers new investors. Although most insurance companies do not practice this approach, it is to be commended. Hopefully, more and more annuity issuers will begin using this renewal rate method.

There is a seven-year penalty period with Future One. The surrender charge is 6% for each of the first three years and then declines by 1% for the next four years. The charge is imposed on redemptions that are in excess of the 10% free withdrawal privilege. Redemptions of any size made after the seventh year are done without an insurance company penalty.

Wisconsin National's Single-Premium Deferred Annuity

Wisconsin National Life
P.O. Box 740
Oshkosh, WI 54902-0740
1/414-235-0800

Rating	A+ (Best), A (Weiss)
Investment options	Rate is only guaranteed for 1 year
Bail-out provisions	None
Free annual withdrawals	10% per year
Minimum guaranteed rate	4%

Company Profile

Wisconsin National Life has been in the insurance business since 1908. The firm's assets, when combined with its parent company,

Nationale Nederlander, are in excess of $140 billion. Wisconsin's own assets, which are in excess of $310 million, are mostly in bonds. Twenty percent of its holdings are in mortgages, and less than 3% of its assets are in high-yield bonds.

This insurance company has a capital surplus of 10% of its assets. This is quite good when compared against an industry average of 6.8%.

Performance

Year	Accumulation Value	Surrender Value
1	$11,000	$10,230
2	$12,060	$11,340
3	$13,180	$12,520
4	$14,360	$13,790
5	$15,640	$15,190

Commentary

At the end of five years, an initial $10,000 grew to $15,640. This represents the second highest accumulation value of any fixed-rate annuity in the study at the end of five years. In 1986, the company's rate was 10.00%; it then dropped to 8.75% by the end of the study in 1991.

Wisconsin National's Single-Premium Deferred Annuity has a penalty period of seven years. The charge for withdrawals in excess of 10% annually starts off at 7% and declines by 1% each year. Redemptions made after the seventh year are not subject to a penalty by Wisconsin National Life.

FPA-82

Sunset Life
3200 Capitol Blvd. South
Olympia, WA 98501-3396
1/800-678-3668

Rating	A+ (Best), A (Weiss)
Investment options	1-year guaranteed rate

Bail-out provisions	There are no withdrawal penalties.
Free annual withdrawals	Money can be taken out twice a year.
Minimum guaranteed rate	4%

Company Profile

Sunset Life was founded in 1937. It has assets of over $300 million. The company has invested 58% of its assets in investment-grade bonds, 13% in mortgages in good standing, 11% in government securities, and 10% in common and preferred stocks.

Performance

Year	Accumulation Value	Surrender Value
1	$10,860	$10,860
2	$11,740	$11,740
3	$12,730	$12,730
4	$13,820	$13,820
5	$14,990	$14,990

Commentary

At the end of five years, an initial $10,000 grew to $14,990. In 1986, the company's rate was 9.00%. After fluctuating a bit, it settled at 8.40% by the end of the study in 1991. The company charges a $15 annual administrative fee.

This is one of the few companies operating that does not impose a penalty for withdrawals made during the first few years of the contract. Thus, investors can take out as much of their investment as they want two times a year without charge or penalty.

AIG's SPDA One-Year Program

AIG Life
1 Alico Plaza, P.O. Box 667

Wilmington, DE 19899
1/800-521-2773

Rating	A (Best), AAA (S&P)
Investment options	1- and 6-year guaranteed rates
Bail-out provisions	Free, if yield falls 1% below initial rate
Free annual withdrawals	10% per year
Minimum guaranteed rate	4%

Company Profile

AIG Life has been in the insurance business since 1962. Its parent company, AIG, has assets in excess of $1 billion. Close to 86% of AIG Life's holdings are in bonds, and 10% are in mortgages. The mortgage portion of AIG's portfolio has performed quite well: 99% of the mortgage loans are performing as expected. The bonds in the portfolio are divided as follows: 63% AAA, 25% AA, 3% AA or BAA, and less than 6% in junk issues.

Performance

Year	Accumulation Value	Surrender Value
1	$10,860	$10,260
2	$11,770	$11,240
3	$12,770	$12,310
4	$13,860	$13,480
5	$14,970	$14,840

Commentary

At the end of five years, an initial $10,000 grew to $14,970. In 1986 the company's rate was 8.50%, where it remained for four years before dropping to 8.00% by the end of the study in 1991.

AIG Life has a six-year penalty period. The surrender charge starts at 6% and declines by 1% each year. Up to 10% of an investment can be taken out each year without penalty or cost.

Kentucky Central's Single-Premium Deferred Annuity

Kentucky Central Life
300 West Vine Street
Lexington, KY 40507
1/800-235-3666

Rating	A− (Best), BBB (S&P)
Investment options	1-year guaranteed rate
Bail-out provisions	None
Free annual withdrawals	10%, 5% penalty first 5 years
Minimum guaranteed rate	4%

Company Profile

This is the oldest life insurer headquartered in the state of Kentucky. The company began operations in 1903. Kentucky Central Life has assets in excess of $1.4 billion. Approximately 42% of its assets are in corporate and government bonds. The company holds no junk bonds. Close to 32% of its portfolio is in mortgages.

Performance

Year	Accumulation Value	Surrender Value
1	$11,020	$10,460
2	$12,040	$11,440
3	$13,160	$12,600
4	$14,380	$13,670
5	$15,680	$14,890

Commentary

At the end of five years, an initial $10,000 grew to $15,680. This represents the highest accumulation value of any fixed-rate annuity in the study. In 1986 the company's rate was 11.00%; it then dropped quickly to 9.30% and then to 9.00% two years later, where it stayed until the end of the study in 1991.

Kentucky Central has a nine-year penalty schedule. The penalty is 5% for the first five years and then declines by 1% for each of the remaining four years. Withdrawals made in the tenth year are not subject to any type of insurance company charge or penalty. The penalty only applies to redemptions that are in excess of the 10% free annual withdrawal privilege.

Horace Mann's Single-Premium Deferred Annuity

Horace Mann Life
1 Horace Mann Plaza
Springfield, IL 62715
1/800-999-1030

Rating	A+ (Best)
Investment options	1-year guaranteed rate
Bail-out provisions	Free, if rate drops below 6.25%
Free annual withdrawals	15% per year for emergencies
Minimum guaranteed rate	5.5% (if single premium deposit)

Company Profile

Horace Mann Life has been in the insurance business since 1945 and has been offering annuities since 1961—the year Congress passed legislation permitting tax-deferred annuities. The company has over 50,000 contract owners who have invested in excess of $1 billion in its annuity programs. The breakdown of its portfolio is 20% government- or agency-backed securities, 35% corporate bonds, 14% mortgage-backed bonds, 12% mortgage loans, 1% foreign bonds, 1% short-term loans, and 1% real estate. The average maturity of its holdings is less than six and a half years. Horace Mann has an A+ rating from A. M. Best.

Performance

Year	Accumulation Value	Surrender Value
1	$10,900	$9,920
2	$11,880	$10,930
3	$12,830	$11,930
4	$13,830	$13,280
5	$14,880	$14,880

Commentary

At the end of five years, an initial $10,000 grew to $14,880. In 1986 the company's rate was 9.00%; it then dropped slowly to 8.00% and again to 7.75%, where it stayed for two years until the end of the study in 1991.

Horace Mann Life has one of the most attractive bailout provisions and annual withdrawal schedules in the event of an emergency. The company describes an emergency as (1) death, (2) three months' continuous disability, or (3) a withdrawal on the renewal date. Redemptions that are not made according to one of these three provisions are subject to a 5% penalty, which declines by 1% annually over a five-year period. These investor-friendly provisions make this an attractive choice.

The company charges a $30 annual fee, which is waived once the contract's cash value equals or exceeds $10,000.

Response 1

Mutual Trust Life
1200 Jorie Blvd.
Oak Brook, IL 60522
1/800-323-7320

Rating	A+ (Best)
Investment options	1-year guaranteed rate
Bail-out provisions	Free, if renewal rate ever falls by 1%

| Free annual withdrawals | 10% per year |
| Minimum guaranteed rate | 4% |

Company Profile

Mutual Trust Life Insurance Company, founded in 1904, is one of the 50 largest mutual life insurance companies in the United States. It has over $500 million of assets and is licensed in 45 states and the District of Columbia. Mutual Trust has over $3 billion of insurance premiums in force and has paid its policy owners dividends every year since 1905. Its portfolio is divided up as follows: 50% bonds, 30% mortgage loans, 10% real estate, and 10% stocks.

Based on its operating performance and financial position, Mutual Trust has received the highest rating for over 25 consecutive years from A. M. Best. Of over 1,800 life insurance companies in the United States, Mutual Trust is one of only 101 that have received an A+ rating every year since 1976, when A. M. Best first began using the letter rating.

Performance

Year	Accumulation Value	Surrender Value
1	$10,900	$10,250
2	$11,820	$11,230
3	$12,850	$12,300
4	$13,970	$13,550
5	$15,120	$14,820

Commentary

At the end of five years, an initial $10,000 grew to $15,120. In 1986 the company's rate was 9.75%; it then quickly dropped to 9.25% and 8.50%, and it dropped once more at the end of the study in 1991 to 8.25%.

During the first year, the contract owner can take out 10% of his or her investment. After the first year, the owner can make annual withdrawals up to 10% of the contract's value. There are no charges for withdrawals after nine years. Withdrawals in excess of 10% during the first nine years are subject to a charge of 9% in the first year. This charge declines by 1% each year until year 10, when no more charges are made.

Response 1 accepts an initial investment as low as $5,000 ($1,800 for qualified money such as retirement plans). It will accept additional contributions of $500 or more during the first policy year only. Thereafter, new money can only be added under a new contract.

American Life's SPDA-4

American Life & Casualty Insurance Company
P.O. Box 9162
Des Moines, IA 50306-9162
1/800-544-0467

Rating	A (Best), A (S&P)
Investment options	1-year guaranteed rate
Bail-out provisions	None
Free annual withdrawals	10% of contract value, any year
Minimum guaranteed rate	5%

Company Profile

American Life was founded in 1951 as the result of the merging of several Midwestern insurance companies. Its total assets are in excess of $2.7 billion. Close to 90% of the company's holdings are in bonds, with 6% in mortgage loans, 2% in stocks, 2% in outstanding policy loans, 0.5% in real estate, and the balance in money market instruments. Less than 4.5% of its assets are in high-yield bonds. The balance of the bond portfolio is in government-backed issues and investment-grade securities.

American Life & Casualty Insurance Company is primarily an issuer of annuities. Due to this specialization, it is able to offer some contract features not commonly seen in other products. For example, SPDA-4 allows the investor a systematic withdrawal plan wherein only the interest is distributed to the contract owner. That leaves the principal intact. Another unique feature is how the company handles its free annual withdrawal privilege. If money is not taken out during the first or second year, the 10% free withdrawal provision becomes cumulative and the client can withdraw 20% the third year, up to 30% the fourth year, 40% during the fifth year, and up to 50% in the sixth year.

Performance

Year	Accumulation Value	Surrender Value
1	$10,950	$10,460
2	$11,830	$11,400
3	$12,800	$12,460
4	$13,900	$13,650
5	$15,060	$14,920

Commentary

At the end of five years, an initial $10,000 grew to $15,060. In 1986 the company's rate was 9.50% and dropped to 8% for the next two years before rising to 8.75% at the end of 1989. By the end of 1989, the rate fell slightly to 8.5% and remained there until the middle of 1991, when it dropped to 8%.

SPDA-4 has an eight-year penalty period that applies to redemptions in excess of the 10% free withdrawal privilege. The penalty is 9.9% for the first year and then declines by 1% for each of the next four years. The penalty for the sixth year is 4.5%, 3% for the seventh year, and 1.5% for the eighth year. Withdrawals made after the eighth year are not subject to a company charge or penalty.

American Life has recently added a medical bail-out provision which states that if you are confined in a hospital or nursing home for 30 days or more, withdrawals of any amount can be made without an insurance company penalty, fee, or charge.

Premier

PFL Life
4333 Edgewood Road, N.E.

Cedar Rapids, IA 52499-0001
1/800-527-2845

Rating	A (Best), AA+ (S&P), AA+ (D&P)
Investment options	None
Bail-out provisions	Free, if rate ever falls below 6%
Free annual withdrawals	10% of contract's value after first year
Minimum guaranteed rate	5.5% for years 2 through 10, 4% thereafter

Company Profile

PFL began operations in 1991. Its parent company, AEGON USA, Inc., is based in the Netherlands. PFL has assets in excess of $3 billion. Close to 51% of its assets are in bonds, 12% is in commercial mortgages, and less than 3% is invested in real estate. The bond holdings are divided into the following categories: 32% AAA or AA, 20% A or BAA, and 25% government bonds.

Performance

Year	Accumulation Value	Surrender Value
1	$10,850	$10,310
2	$11,770	$11,240
3	$12,770	$12,200
4	$13,860	$13,480
5	$15,040	$14,770

Commentary

At the end of five years, an initial $10,000 grew to $15,040. In 1986 the company's rate was 8.50%, where it remained for the next five years.

CHAPTER 15

The 10 Best Variable Annuities

This chapter covers the 10 best-performing variable annuities in the following categories: growth, aggressive growth, growth and income, international stocks, balanced, corporate bond, global and international bonds, and high-yield bonds.

Each of the variable annuities reviewed in this chapter is ranked either excellent, very good, good, fair, or poor in each of the following categories: total return, risk-adjusted return, portfolio diversification, performance predictability, management expenses, insurance costs, and surrender charges. A ranking of "good" means that the annuity ranks slightly above average compared to its peer group.

> *Total return* refers to the subaccounts' performance over the past three and/or five years. Performance was the sole criteria for whether or not a variable annuity was included in this chapter. A 10-year time horizon was not used, since only a handful of variable accounts have been in existence that long. Performance over one year was not used, since such figures could be the result of either luck or a nonrecurring event.
>
> *Risk-adjusted return* looks at how well an account performed, based on the amount of risk it took. If an account receives high marks on a risk-adjusted basis, this means that the fund took X amount of risk but received an $X + Y$ rate of return. A

portfolio that is rated poorly in this area may still have good results but took higher than normal risks, compared to its peer group. You should not necessarily avoid those variable annuities that are rated either "fair" or "poor" in the risk-adjusted return category; a higher than normal risk can be offset by a low-risk investment in your portfolio mix.

Portfolio diversification shows how well, or poorly, the account is spread out (invested) in different securities and industry groups.

Performance predictability has to do with the stability or range of returns. Many investors are simply concerned with the bottom line: "How much did I make?" Others want more reassurance as to what they can expect. For the moderate or more conservative customer, this ranking will be of value.

Management expenses indicate how well an account is run. These costs include what the subaccount is paying out in fees to those who oversee your money as well as administrative expenses (overhead, staff, research, etc.). The performance figures cited throughout this book are always net of any management expenses.

Insurance costs have to do with the guaranteed death benefit or mortality fee. Some insurers charge a higher than normal fee for such protection; others are more reasonable. The difference between a "high" and "low" fee is very small, often only one or two tenths of a percentage point (and never greater than $1/2\%$).

Surrender charges are also shown. They indicate exactly what it would cost to liquidate the account. As you may recall, a surrender charge can be avoided by one of the following: (1) death, (2) disability, (3) annuitization, (4) limiting withdrawals to 10% a year, or (5) waiting for the surrender period to end.

Additional Information

As you read through each of these 10 descriptions, you will notice that background information about the management is given as well as some comparison figures. Note that the typical variable annuity charges an investor 1.26% of his or her contract's value each year for the guaranteed death benefit. Some of the annuities listed charge more, some less. The cost is spelled out under the "Administrative Costs" and "Insurance Costs" sections. Finally, each subaccount description ends by showing you the other portfolios available within the "family" as well as the average annual return for each of these portfolios over the past three years (shown in parentheses).

Equitable Equi-Vest Aggressive Stock

The Equitable
P.O. Box 2996 GPO
New York, NY 10119-2996
1/800-628-6673

Total return	Excellent
Risk-adjusted return	Excellent
Portfolio diversification	Very good
Performance predictability	Poor
Management expenses	Excellent
Insurance costs	Fair
Surrender charges	6% level for 6 years

Total Return

Over the past five years, Equi-Vest Aggressive Stock portfolio has taken $10,000 and turned it into $27,630 ($27,990 over three years). This translates into an average compound annual return of 22.5% over five years and 41% over the past three years. The average aggressive growth portfolio had annualized returns over the past three and five years of 21.8% and 13.9%, respectively.

A $10,000 investment in the fund at its May 1, 1984 inception was worth over $50,600 at the beginning of 1992. This translates into an average compound rate of 25.5% per year.

Year:	1984	1985	1986	1987	1988	1989	1990	1991
Return:	+5%	+43%	+22%	-1%	0	+43%	+6%	+85%

Management

This $1 billion portfolio has been managed by Barry R. Feirstein since 1987. Barry joined the company in 1978, starting off as a stock analyst, specializing in technology issues. He became a portfolio manager in 1984. There are over 90 different stocks in this portfolio.

Equi-Vest is sold only by registered representatives of The Equitable. It is not available through other brokers. Equitable has an A. M. Best rating of A − , A from Standard & Poor's, A from Duff & Phelps, and A3 from Moody's.

Administrative and Insurance Costs

The average aggressive growth portfolio has an annual management expense of 0.65%. Equi-Vest Aggressive Stock portfolio charges its investors 0.55% for management and fund expenses and 1.34% annually for insurance. Thus, its fees are less than average when it comes to management and administrative costs but somewhat higher than normal when it comes to insurance fees.

Surrender Charges

Equi-Vest imposes a flat 6% charge for withdrawals during the first six years of the investment. Thereafter, the contract owner is free to make withdrawals of any size without incurring a company penalty. There is also a $30 annual contract fee.

Other Investment Options within the Family

Other portfolio options available within this variable annuity family include Balanced (19.8%), Common Stock (15.2%), and Money Market (6.4%).

American Skandia A.S.A.P.
Alger Small Capitalization

> American Skandia Life Assurance Corporation
> Tower One Corporate Drive
> Shelton, CT 06484
> 1/800-752-6342

Total return	Excellent
Risk-adjusted return	Excellent
Portfolio diversification	Excellent
Performance predictability	Fair
Management expenses	Fair
Insurance costs	Fair
Surrender charges	7% declining for 7 years

Total Return

Over the past three years, American Skandia's Small Cap portfolio has taken $10,000 and turned it into $26,870. This translates into an average compound annual return of 39.2% over the past three years. The average aggressive growth portfolio had annualized returns of 21.8% over the past three years.

A $10,000 investment in the fund at its September, 1988 inception was worth over $25,990 at the beginning of 1992; the fund has had a cumulative return of 160% since its beginning. This translates into an average compound rate of 33.2% per year.

Year:	1988	1989	1990	1991
Return:	−4%	+62%	+7%	+55%

Management

This $38 million portfolio has been managed by Fred Alger Management Company since its inception. David Alger, age 48, is the portfolio manager of every Alger fund. Fred is the president and CEO of the company. David received his undergraduate degree from Harvard and an MBA from the University of Michigan.

The firm is guided by the philosophy that "companies with certain identifiable characteristics make excellent candidates for dynamic growth." The company generates its own research. Its computer system tracks over 1,400 firms. The analyst who researches the stock is the one who recommends it, tracks its performance, and decides when to sell it.

Fred Alger's management analysis techniques enable the company to spot stocks at a formative stage with a high degree of accuracy—before other investors recognize them as "surprise situations." This early response to investment opportunities is what Alger calls the "serendipitous factor."

Skandia has an A+ rating from A. M. Best and an AA rating from Standard & Poor's.

Administrative and Insurance Costs

The average aggressive growth portfolio has an annual management expense of 0.65%. Alger Small Capitalization portfolio charges its investors 1.06% for management and fund expenses and 1.40% annually for insurance. Thus, its fees are high for a variable annuity contract.

Surrender Charges

Skandia imposes a 7% penalty for the first year of the investment; thereafter, the penalty decreases by 1% per year for six more years. Thereafter, the contract owner is free to make withdrawals of any size without incurring a company penalty. There is also a $30 annual contract fee.

Other Investment Options
within the Family

Other portfolio options available within this variable annuity family include Alger American Growth (20.1%), Alger American Income & Growth (8.7%), Henderson International Growth (11%), Neuberger & Berman Balanced (12.6%), Neuberger & Berman Growth (13.9%), and Neuberger & Berman Limited Maturity Bond (8.6%). Skandia now offers three additional subaccounts (short-term global bond, growth, and growth and income) managed by the Alliance mutual fund group.

Kemper Advantage III
Total Return

Kemper Investors Life Insurance Company
120 South La Salle

Chicago, IL 60603
1/800-621-5001

Total return	Excellent
Risk-adjusted return	Very good
Portfolio diversification	Excellent
Performance predictability	Excellent
Management expenses	Excellent
Insurance costs	Fair
Surrender charges	6% declining for 6 years

Total Return

Over the past five years, Kemper Advantage III Total Return portfolio has taken $10,000 and turned it into $17,260 ($18,790 for three years). This translates into an average compound annual return of 20% over the past three years and 13.5% for the last five years. The average balanced portfolio had annualized returns over the past three and five years of 13.1% and 10.8%, respectively.

A $10,000 investment in the fund at its March 5, 1982, inception was worth over $34,160 at the beginning of 1992. This translates into an average compound rate of 13.3% per year.

Year:	1982	1983	1984	1985	1986	1987	1988	1989	1990	1991
Return:	+18%	+12%	−5%	+27%	+14%	−1%	+10%	+22%	+4%	+36%

Management

This $450 million portfolio has been managed by Gordon P. Wilson since its 1982 inception. Gordon has managed Kemper Total Return since 1972, a number-one ranked mutual fund. He has also managed a gold fund for Kemper and continues to manage its international stock fund while acting as the company's international division president. Wilson joined Kemper in 1966 as an analyst and became an analyst supervisor in 1971. He received his undergraduate degree in economics in 1963 and was awarded an M.A. in finance from the University of Illinois. Gordon is a chartered financial analyst (CFA).

Kemper has an A rating from A. M. Best, an A+ from Duff & Phelps, and an A2 rating from Moody's.

Administrative and Insurance Costs

The average balanced portfolio has an annual management expense of 0.82%. This balanced portfolio charges its investors 0.61% for management and fund expenses and 1.30% annually for insurance. Thus, its total fees are lower than its peer group average.

Surrender Charges

Kemper III starts off with a 6% penalty for the first year of the investment; thereafter the penalty declines by 1% for five more years. Thereafter, the contract owner is free to make withdrawals of any size without incurring a company penalty. There is also a $25 annual contract fee.

Other Investment Options
Within the Family

Other portfolio options available within this variable annuity family include Equity (25.5%), Government Securities (11.4%), High Yield (6.8%), and Money Market (6.3%). The company now also offers an international portfolio.

Equitable Equi-Vest Balanced

The Equitable
P.O. Box 2996 GPO
New York, NY 10116-2996
1/800-628-6673

Total return	Excellent
Risk-adjusted return	Very good
Portfolio diversification	Excellent
Performance predictability	Excellent

Management expenses	Excellent
Insurance costs	Poor
Surrender charges	6% fixed for 6 years

Total Return

Over the past five years, Equitable Equi-Vest Balanced portfolio has taken $10,000 and turned it into $18,600 ($17,330 for three years). This translates into an average compound annual return of 20% over the past three years and 13% for the last five years.

A $10,000 investment in the fund at its May, 1984 inception was worth over $27,350 at the beginning of 1992. This translates into an average compound rate of 14% per year.

Year:	1984	1985	1986	1987	1988	1989	1990	1991
Return:	+6%	+24%	+12%	−5%	+13%	+25%	−1%	+40%

Management

This $1 billion portfolio has been managed by Judith A. Taylor since 1988. Judith has been with Equitable since 1969. She has a B.A. and M.B.A. from the University of Pittsburgh.

There are over 100 different securities in this portfolio. Approximately 60% of its holdings are in common stocks, with 27% in bonds, 7% in money market instruments, and 6% in convertible securities. The fixed-income portion of the portfolio has an average maturity of 26 years and a quality rating of AA+.

The Equitable was founded in 1859. It has over $140 billion in assets under management and is ranked as one of the three largest insurance companies in the country. Equitable has an A. M. Best rating of A −, A from Standard & Poor's, A from Duff & Phelps, and A3 from Moody's.

Administrative and Insurance Costs

The average balanced portfolio has an annual management expense of 0.82%. This balanced portfolio charges its investors 0.45% for management and fund expenses and 1.49% annually for insurance. Thus, its fees are slightly lower than its peer group average.

Surrender Charges

Equi-Vest Balanced has a 6% penalty, which remains level for all six years. Thereafter, the contract owner is free to make withdrawals of any size without incurring a company penalty. There is also a $30 annual contract fee.

Other Investment Options within the Family

Other portfolio options available within this variable annuity family include Aggressive Stock (40.8%), Common Stock (15.2%), and Money Market (6.4%).

Great American Reserve VA Bond

Great American Reserve Insurance Company
16415 Addison Road, Suite 315
Dallas, TX. 75248
1/800-866-2776

Total return	Excellent
Risk-adjusted return	Fair
Portfolio diversification	Fair
Performance predictability	Excellent
Management expenses	Excellent
Insurance costs	Very good
Surrender charges	8% declining for 8 years

Total Return

Over the past five years, Great American Reserve VA Bond portfolio has taken $10,000 and turned it into $15,830 ($14,500 for three years). This translates into an average compound annual return of 13% over the past three years and 9.6% for the last five years. The average corporate bond portfolio had annualized returns over the past three and five of 10.4% and 7.8%, respectively.

A $10,000 investment in the fund at its 1981 inception was

worth over $35,200 at the beginning of 1992. This translates into an average compound rate of 12% per year.

Year:	1981	1982	1983	1984	1985	1986	1987	1988	1989	1990	1991
Return:	+14%	+23%	+9%	+12%	+16%	+12%	+2%	+7%	+14%	+6%	+20%

Management

The portfolio has been managed by Gregory J. Hahn and Burt Guiterrez since 1990. Burt has been with Great American for close to five years and heads the corporate trading desk. Previously, he was with Kidder Peabody. Burt is a CFA and graduated with a B.S. from Wharton. Greg is also a CFA and has been with the company for three years. He is the senior analyst responsible for the firm's analytical group. Greg has a B.A. from the University of Wisconsin and an M.B.A. from Indiana University. Assets are managed using a management team approach, both in style and philosophy.

Great American Reserve is licensed to do business in 47 states and the District of Columbia. It carries an A+ rating from A. M. Best, a B− from Weiss, and a BBq from S&P.

Administrative and Insurance Costs

The average corporate bond portfolio has an annual management expense of 0.65%. This corporate bond portfolio charges its investors 0.30% for management and fund expenses and 1.05% annually for insurance. Thus, its fees are much lower than the majority of variable annuity contracts.

Surrender Charges

Reserve VA Bond has an 8% penalty, which declines by 1% annually for eight years. Thereafter, the contract owner is free to make withdrawals of any size without incurring a company penalty. There is also a $20 annual contract fee.

Other Investment Options
within the Family

Other portfolio options available within this variable annuity family include Stock (20%) and Money Market (6.7%).

Kemper Advantage III Equity

KILICO
P.O. Box 4553
Chicago, IL 60680-9677
1/800-621-5001

Total return	Excellent
Risk-adjusted return	Very good
Portfolio diversification	Excellent
Performance predictability	Very good
Management expenses	Very good
Insurance costs	Fair
Surrender charges	6% declining for 6 years

Total Return

Over the past five years, Kemper Advantage III Equity portfolio has taken $10,000 and turned it into $20,440 ($20,140 for three years). This translates into an average compound annual return of 26% over the past three years and 15.4% for the past five years. The average growth portfolio had an annualized return of 16.8% over the past three years.

A $10,000 investment in the fund at its December, 1983 inception was worth over $29,600 at the beginning of 1992. This translates into an average compound rate of 14.4% per year.

Year:	1984	1985	1986	1987	1988	1989	1990	1991
Return:	+9%	+23%	+8%	+.5%	+1%	+27%	+1%	+57%

Management

This $65 million portfolio has been managed by C. Beth Cotner since 1984. Beth has been a money manager with Kemper since 1984. She has managed Total Return since 1986 and also manages Summit, both of which are part of the Kemper mutual fund family. Altogether, she manages over $800 million for the company. Beth graduated Phi Beta Kappa from Ohio State and has an M.B.A. from George Washington University.

Kemper has an A rating from A. M. Best, an A+ from Duff & Phelps, and an A2 rating from Moody's.

Administrative and Insurance Costs

The average growth portfolio has an annual management expense of 0.71%. This growth portfolio charges its investors 0.7% for management and fund expenses and 1.30% annually for insurance. Thus, its fees are just a little bit higher than its peer group average. There is also a $25 annual contract fee.

Surrender Charges

Advantage III Equity has a 6% penalty, which declines by 1% each year for seven years. Thereafter, the contract owner is free to make withdrawals of any size without incurring a company penalty.

Other Investment Options within the Family

Other portfolio options available within this variable annuity family include Government Securities (11.4%), High Yield (6.8%), Total Return (20%), and Money Market (6.3%).

Aetna VA Account C Variable Fund

Aetna Life Insurance and Annuity Company
151 Farmington Avenue
Hartford, CT 06156
1/203-273-7108

Total return	Excellent
Risk-adjusted return	Fair
Portfolio diversification	Excellent

Performance	Excellent
predictability	
Management expenses	Excellent
Insurance costs	Good
Surrender charges	5% declining for 10 years

Total Return

Over the past five years, Aetna VA Account C Variable Fund port-folio has taken $10,000 and turned it into $19,030 ($16,190 for three years). This translates into an average compound annual return of 17% over the past three years, 13.7% for the last five years. The average growth and income portfolio had annualized returns over the past 3, 5, and 10 years of 13.2%, 12.2%, and 16.8%, respectively.

A $10,000 investment in the portfolio at its 1984 inception was worth over $30,680 at the beginning of 1992. This translates into an average compound rate of 15% per year.

Year:	1984	1985	1986	1987	1988	1989	1990	1991
Return:	+6%	+30%	+17%	+4%	+13%	+27%	+2%	+25%

Unlike eight of the other variable annuity accounts shown in this chapter, this particular portfolio only accepts money from qualified retirement plans (IRAs, pension plans, TSAs, etc.).

Management

This $1.8 billion portfolio is managed by Charles N. Dawkins, Martin Duffy, John Shay, Neil E. Yarhouse, and Richard A. DiChillo. Charles, a CFA, has an A.B. from Harvard and a total of 31 years of investment experience. Charles has been the head of Aetna's Annuity Investment Department since 1970. Martin, a CFA, has a B.A. in finance from the University of Notre Dame and an M.B.A. from the University of Connecticut. Martin joined Aetna in 1972 and has served as both a trader and as an analyst. He is responsible for technology, consumer durable goods, and banking equities. John, a CFA, has a B.S. from the New Mexico Institute of Mining and Technology. John joined Aetna in 1974. He was an assistant director of research at The Bank of New York before coming to Aetna. John's areas of responsibility include nondurable goods, health care, and transportation securities. Neil has a B.A. from Pennsylvania State University and an M.B.A. from the Wharton School. He joined Aetna 10 years ago and has a total of 27 years of investment experience. Previously, he was the senior portfolio manager at Colonial Bank. Neil oversees energy and machinery equity investments. Richard, a CFA, has a B.S. from Bryant College and an M.B.A. from Rensselaer Polytechnic Institute. His 11 years of investment experience have all been with Aetna. Richard is responsible for the insurance, retailing, utility, and media equities.

Administrative and Insurance Costs

The average growth and income portfolio has an annual management expense of 0.52%. This growth and income portfolio charges its investors 0.3% for management and fund expenses and 1.25% annually for insurance. Thus, its fees are lower than its peer group average. There is also a $20 annual contract fee.

Surrender Charges

C Variable Fund has a 5% penalty for the first four years, a 4% penalty for the next two years, a 3% penalty for the following two years, and a 2% penalty for the ninth and tenth years. Thereafter, the contract owner is free to make withdrawals of any size without incurring a company penalty.

Other Investment Options within the Family

Other portfolio options available within this variable annuity family include Income Shares (12.9%) and Investment Advisers Fund (N/A).

American Legacy II High-Yield Bond

Lincoln National Life Insurance Co.
P.O. Box 2348
Fort Wayne, IN 46801
1/800-443-8137

Total return	Excellent
Risk-adjusted return	Not available
Portfolio diversification	Not available
Performance predictability	Excellent
Management expenses	Very good
Insurance costs	Fair
Surrender charges	6% declining for 7 years

Total Return

Over the past five years, American Legacy II High-Yield Bond portfolio has taken $10,000 and turned it into $16,175 ($13,900 for three years). This translates into an average compound annual return of 12% over the past three years (10.1% for five years). The average high-yield portfolio had annualized returns over the past three and five years of 7.3% and 6.4%, respectively.

A $10,000 investment in the fund at its February, 1984 inception was worth over $25,800 at the beginning of 1992. This translates into an average compound rate of 12.7% per year. This is one of the few mutual funds or variable annuities concentrating in high-yield bonds, which has shown positive results every year since inception.

Year:	1984	1985	1986	1987	1988	1989	1990	1991
Return:	+9%	+24%	+18%	+3%	+13%	+9%	+2%	+25%

Management

This $115 million portfolio has been managed by Capital Guardian Trust Company since its inception. The Capital organization began operations in 1931. The company has offices in Los Angeles, San Francisco, New York, Washington, D.C., London, Geneva, Singapore, Hong Kong, and Tokyo. The firm, which manages over $25 billion, spends over $30 million a year on research. Of the 119 key decision-making investment people who have joined Capital in the past 20 years, 89 are still with the organization. There are 31 portfolio managers who oversee mutual funds, pension plans, and variable annuities. Of these 31 managers, 24 have been with Capital for more than 10 years and 11 have been with the company for more than 20 years.

Administrative and Insurance Costs

The average high-yield portfolio has an annual management expense of 0.88%. This high-yield portfolio charges its investors 0.68% for management and portfolio expenses and 1.35% annually for insurance. Thus, its fees are almost identical to its peer group average. There is also a $35 annual contract fee.

Surrender Charges

Legacy II High-Yield Bond has a 6% penalty for the first two years, which declines by 1% each year for an additional five years. Thereafter, the contract owner is free to make withdrawals of any size without incurring a company penalty.

Other Investment Options
Within the Family

Other portfolio options available within this variable annuity family include Growth (17.5%), Growth and Income (13.5%), U.S. Government/AAA Securities (10.5%), and Cash Management (6%).

MFS/Sun (US) Compass G
Worldwide Governments

Sun Life Annuity Service Center
P.O. Box 1024
Boston, MA 02103
1/800-752-7216

Total return	Excellent
Risk-adjusted return	Fair
Portfolio diversification	Poor
Performance predictability	Excellent

Management expenses	Poor
Insurance costs	Fair
Surrender charges	6% declining for 7 years

Total Return

Over the past three years, MFS/Sun (US) Compass G Worldwide Governments portfolio has taken $10,000 and turned it into $13,840. This translates into an average compound annual return of 11.4%. The average international bond portfolio had annualized returns over the past three and five years of 10.6% and 11.9%, respectively. This particular portfolio can only be used by qualified plans.

A $10,000 investment in the fund at its July, 1986 inception was worth over $13,840 at the beginning of 1992. This translates into an average compound rate of 12% per year.

Year:	1986	1987	1988	1989	1990	1991
Return:	+6%	+23%	+3%	+6%	+16%	+12%

Management

This $1.6 million portfolio has been managed by Leslie Nanberg since its 1986 inception. Leslie also manages MIT Total Return and MFS World Government Series, both members of the MFS mutual fund family. He received both an undergraduate and graduate degree from Northwestern University. Lesley has been with MFS since 1980, first becoming an assistant vice president of investments in 1981, moving up to vice president in 1983, and then senior vice president in 1986. Leslie is a CFA.

MFS has a Standard & Poor's rating of AAA and an A+ rating from A. M. Best.

Administrative and Insurance Costs

The average international bond portfolio has an annual management expense of 0.75%. This international bond portfolio charges its investors 0.75% for management and fund expenses and 1.30% annually for insurance. There is also a $25 annual contract fee.

Surrender Charges

Worldwide Governments has a 6% penalty, which remains fixed for the first two years. The surrender charge then declines by 1% annually. Thereafter, the contract owner is free to make withdrawals of any size without incurring a company penalty.

Other Investment Options within the Family

Other portfolio options available within this variable annuity family include Capital Appreciation Series (21.8%), Government Securities Series (11.1%), High-Yield Series (6.5%), Mass Capital Development (13.1%), Mass Financial Bond (11.5%), Mass Financial Total Return (12.1%), Mass Investors (18.8%), Mass Investors Growth Stock (22.6%), and Money Market Series (6.2%).

Charter/Scudder Horizon International

Scudder Horizon
175 Federal Street
Boston, MA 02110
1/800-225-2470

Total return	Very good
Risk-adjusted return	Good
Portfolio diversification	Fair
Performance predictability	Very good
Management expenses	Fair
Insurance costs	Excellent
Surrender charges	No surrender charge

Total Return

Over the past three years, Charter/Scudder Horizon International portfolio has taken $10,000 and turned it into $13,998. This translates into an average compound annual return of 11.3%. The average international stock portfolio had a 7.7% annualized return over the past three years.

A $10,000 investment in the fund at its October, 1988 inception was worth over $14,160 at the beginning of 1992.

Year:	1989	1990	1991
Return:	+37%	−9%	+11%

Management

This $8 million portfolio has been managed by Carol Franklin since 1989. Carol received her undergraduate degree from Smith College in 1975 and an M.B.A. from Columbia in 1980. She joined Scudder in 1987. Prior to working for Scudder, Carol worked for The Boston Co. and Bank of America. She is a CFA.

Administrative and Insurance Costs

This international stock portfolio charges its investors 1.50% for management and fund expenses and 0.70% annually for insurance. Thus, its total fees are quite a bit lower than its peer group average. There is no annual contract fee.

Surrender Charges

Horizon International has no surrender charges. The contract owner is free to make withdrawals of any size, at any time, without incurring a company penalty.

Other Investment Options within the Family

Other portfolio options available within this variable annuity family include Bond (11.4%), Capital Growth (15.5%), Diversified (13.1%), and Money Market (6.5%).

APPENDIX A

Sources of Additional Information

This book should answer every question you might have about both fixed-rate and variable annuities. But no matter how thorough it might be, it cannot provide you with ongoing performance figures, future ratings of companies, new products, or additional features offered by existing companies. Therefore, you may wish to subscribe to or contact one or more of the sources listed in this appendix. Most, if not all, of these analytical sources will send you a free sample copy of their publication.

A. M. Best

The Best publication comes out semiannually and costs only $50. The service prints annual reports that detail the total net assets of annuity companies. The publication also includes outlines of the various products, their contract features, and expenses. Best may be contacted at (908)439-2200 or by writing to A. M. Best Co., Customer Service, A. M. Best Road, Oldwick, NJ, 08858.

Annuity Review Board

The Annuity Review Board provides detailed financial information regarding the financial structure of most well-known insurance companies. This information is compiled from various sources and in most cases is verified with the insurance company directly.

The Annuity Review Board also reviews policy provisions for individual annuity policies, whether fixed or variable, and allows the policy holder to evaluate these provisions in an objective manner. Such information is compiled and then verified with the marketing department to ensure that correct information is being reported. In many cases, the information provided exceeds the data available in the prospectus.

The Annuity Review Board does not provide advice or recommendations, nor does it offer for sale any annuity policy. The information is provided for a nominal fee and can be obtained by calling (602) 953-0599 or writing The Annuity Review Board, 3835 North 32nd Street, Suite 6, Phoenix, AZ 85018.

Lipper

The Lipper Variable Insurance Products Performance Analysis Service includes total return performance rankings for current and historic periods such as monthly, annual, two-, three-, four-, and five-year periods. Lipper may be contacted by telephoning (303)534-3472 or (201)273-2772 or by writing to Lipper Analytical Services, Inc., 47 Maple Street, Summit, NJ 07901.

Morningstar

Morningstar has recently added a separate service devoted solely to variable annuities. The publication, *Variable Annuity Performance Report*, is printed monthly. The service covers over 700 subaccounts and posts performance figures ranging from one month to 10 years. A separate section lists the advisor's name and phone number, surrender charges, fund and insurance expense ratios, turnover ratios, quarter-end net assets, income ratios, and, for the statistically minded, the alpha, beta, and R-squared of each subaccount. A one-year subscription costs $125. Morningstar can be contacted by telephoning (800)876-5005 or by writing to Morningstar, 53 West Jackson Blvd., Chicago, IL 60604.

S&P Stock Guide

Virtually every brokerage firm in the nation has at least one copy of the *S&P Stock Guide*. At the back of each stock guide is a listing of several dozen variable annuity products. Performance figures are for year-to-date for one, two, three, and four years. The service costs $118 annually and is published monthly. Their address is Standard & Poor's Corp., Publishers, 25 Broadway, New York, NY 10004 (1-800-221-5222).

VARDS

VARDS reports come out monthly; an annual subscription costs $698. The company also publishes an annual almanac for $50. The service includes past performance figures for various periods and also ranks the top-performing portfolios against their respective peer group. Performance figures are independently calculated by VARDS. Return figures are also included for those variable contracts that include one or more fixed-rate subaccounts. The almanac includes informative articles, an extensive directory, and performance figures on close to 600 variable contracts. VARDS may be contacted by telephoning (305)252-4600 or writing to Financial Planning Resources, Inc., P.O. Box 161998, Miami, FL 33116.

Periodicals

Financial Planning Magazine, based in New York City, annually publishes an extensive survey of annuities' performance and costs. *Barron's* also publishes week-to-week values for variable annuities.

Directory

Table A.1 lists insurance company names, product names, and telephone numbers of those companies that issue variable annuities.

**Table A.1 *Names, Products, and Telephone Numbers
of Companies Issuing Variable Annuities***

Company	Contract Name	Telephone
AETNA Life Ins. and Annuity Co.	Variable Annuity Account C	203-273-3691
AIG Life Insurance Company	The Variable Annuity	800-441-7468
Amer. Cap/Nationwide Life Ins. Co.	The Investment Annuity	800-421-5666
Amer. Intern'l Life Assur. Co. of N.Y.	The Variable Annuity	800-441-7468
Amer. Skandia Life Assur. Corp.	LifeVest & A.S.A.P.	800-752-6342
Amer. United Life Insurance Co.	AUL American	317-263-1877
Ameritas Variable Life Ins. Co.	Overture Annuity I & II	800-634-8353
Anchor Nat'l Life Ins. Co.	American Pathway II & ICAP II	800-445-7861
Bankers Nat'l Life Insurance Co.	Series 2000	800-888-4918
Bankers Security Life Ins. Society	The USA Plan	800-338-7737
Canada Life Ins. Co. of America	VariFund Annuity	800-333-2542
Charter Nat'l Life Ins. Co.	Helmsman	800-325-8405
Colonial/John Hancock Mutual Life	Colonial/Hancock Liberty Ann.	800-338-1589
Confederation Life Ins. & Ins. Co.	MultiVest Plan	800-548-8648
Connecticut Mutual Life Ins. Co.	Panorama	800-243-2501
Dreyfus/Mutual Benefit Life Ins. Co.	Dreyfus Series 2000 Deferred	800-334-6899
The Equitable	EQUI-VEST	800-628-6673

(continued)

Table A.1 *Names, Products, and Telephone Numbers of Companies Issuing Variable Annuities (cont.)*

Company	Contract Name	Telephone
Family Life Ins. Co.	Portfolio Plus	800-523-0273
Fidelity and Guaranty Life Ins. Co.	F&G Variable Annuity	301-547-3000
Fidelity Investments Life Ins. Co.	Fidelity Retirement Reserves	800-554-6666
First Capital Life Ins. Co.	Shearson VIP	619-452-9060
First Variable Life Ins. Co.	VISTA (Funds A and E)	800-228-1035
The Franklin Life Ins. Co.	Franklin Var. Ann. Funds A,B,C	217-528-2011
The Golden American Life Ins. Co.	The Specialty Manager	800-447-3644
Great American Reserve Ins. Co.	MaxiFlex Comb. Fixed & Var.	800-866-2776
Great-West Life & Annuity Ins. Co.	MAXIM	800-228-8706
Guardian Ins. and Annuity Co.	Value Guard I and Value Guard II	800-221-3253
Guardian Ins. and Annuity Co.	Guardian Investor	800-221-3253
The Hartford Life Ins. Co.	The Director	800-862-6668
The Hartford Life Ins. Co.	Putnam Capital Manager	800-862-6668
IDS Life Ins. Co.	Flexible Annuity Life	612-372-3131
Investors Life Ins. Co. of N. Amer.	CIGNA Variable Annuity	215-351-2900
John Hancock Mutual Life Ins. Co.	Accommodator & Independence	617-572-9950
John Hancock Mutual Life Ins. Co.	Accommodator 2000	617-572-9950

**Table A.1   Names, Products, and Telephone Numbers
of Companies Issuing Variable Annuities (cont.)**

Company	Contract Name	Telephone
Kemper Investors Life Ins. Co.	Advantage III	800-554-5426
Keyport Life Ins. Co.	Keyflex 1 and Keyflex 4	800-437-4466
The Life Ins. Co. of Virginia	Asset Allocation Annuity	804-281-6000
Lincoln Nat'l Life Ins. Co.	MultiFund	800-348-1212
Lincoln Nat'l Life Ins. Co.	The American Legacy II	800-348-1212
The Manufacturers Life Ins. Co.	Manulife Financial Var. Ann.	416-926-6700
Merrill Lynch (see Family Life)		
Metropolitan Life Ins. Co.	VestMet	800-223-3370
MFS/SUN Life Assurance Co.	Compass I, II, & III	800-343-2829
MFS/SUN Life Assurance Co.	MFS Regatta	800-343-2829
The Minnesota Mutual Life Ins. Co.	MultiOption	612-298-3887
Monarch Life Ins. Co.	MILESTONE (Fund VA)	800-228-1035
MONY Life Ins. Co. of America	The MONYMaster	800-792-6669
Nationwide Life Ins. Co.	Best of America III & IV	800-321-6064
The New England Mut. Life Ins Co.	Zenith Accumulator	617-578-2000
North American Life & Casualty Co	Franklin Valuemark II	800-542-5427
N. American Security Life Ins. Co.	Venture Comb. Fixed/ Var. Ann.	800-344-1029
Northwestern Mutual Life Ins. Co.	NML Variable Annuity Acc't. B	414-271-1444

Table A.1 *Names, Products, and Telephone Numbers of Companies Issuing Variable Annuities (cont.)*

Company	Contract Name	Telephone
Penn Mutual Life Ins. Co.	Diversifier II	800-873-6285
Phoenix Mutual Life Ins. Co.	The Big Edge Plus	800-243-4361
PRUCO Life Ins. Co.	Discovery Plus	201-877-2000
The Prudential Ins. Co. of America	Discovery Plus & VIP	201-802-2000
SAFECO Life Ins. Co.	Resource Variable Account B	800-426-7649
Scudder, Stevens & Clark, Inc.	Scudder Horizon	800-225-2470
Security Benefit Life Ins. Co.	Variflex	800-888-2461
Security First Life Ins. Co.	Investor's Choice	800-225-8899
Seligman Marketing, Inc.	Seligman Mutual Benefit Plan	800-221-2783
Sentry Life Ins. Co.	The Patriot	800-533-7827
SMA Life Assurance Co.	SMA Variable Annuity	508-852-1000
Smith Barney/ Nationwide Life Ins.	Portfolio Foundation	212-698-5349
Southwestern Life Ins. Co.	Variable Annuity Fund I	800-468-3863
Templeton/Phoenix Mutual Life	Templeton Invest. Plus (TIP)	800-237-0738
The Travelers Ins. Co.	The Universal Annuity	203-277-0111
Union Central Life Ins. Co.	Carillon Account	513-595-2600
Western Reserve Life Assur. Co.	WRL Freedom Variable Ann.	800-237-8337

APPENDIX B

Calculating Your Returns

One of the most publicized features of an annuity is its ability to grow and compound tax deferred. Qualified retirement plans, such as IRAs, Keoghs, pension and profit-sharing plans, as well as 401(k) and 403(b) plans are the only other type of investment vehicle in which money can grow on a tax-deferred basis.

Unfortunately, the amount you can contribute to a retirement plan is limited each year. This is not the case with annuities. You can invest an unlimited amount of money in an annuity at any time. There is no annual limit. In fact, annuities are among the few tax-advantaged vehicles left. A few tax shelters still exist, but none of them is easily marketable—and the great majority of them have a very poor track record.

Before we can see the effects of tax-deferred growth, we must first learn how to use the tables found in Appendix C. Each table is differentiated by an interest rate figure. The first table is marked "Rate 5%"; the second table is "Rate 6%," and so on. Each table contains four subtables. The description of each subtable is exactly the same from page to page; only the assumed interest rate or factor changes.

Turn to Appendix C, and let us see how these tables work and how they apply not only to annuities, but also to everyday life.

Table 1: Compounding Factor

This is the subtable you will use most frequently. It shows what you will end up with after a specific number of years, *assuming a certain rate of return.*

For example, turn to the table titled "Rate 7%" in Appendix C (Table C.3). Focus on the column marked "Table 1," which is described as "What an initial amount becomes when growing at compound interest." Let us assume that you have $20,000 to invest in a fixed-rate annuity that has a guaranteed rate of 7% for 10 years. You want to know what your $20,000 will be worth at the end of this period. By looking under "Table 1" until you match it with the *row* identified as "Year 10," you will see the number 1.97. It is this number, or factor, that you multiply by your original investment, $20,000 in this example. The resulting figure, $39,400, is what $20,000 grows to at the end of 10 years, assuming a 7% growth rate (1.97 times $20,000).

Let us go through one more example before moving on to the second table. Assume that you have just received a gift of $58,240. You want to invest this money in a variable annuity. In particular, you are interested in a subaccount within the variable annuity that has averaged 15% annually over the past several years. You decide to invest the $58,240 in this growth portfolio and are willing to leave the money there for the next six years.

Assuming the investment grows at 15% annually, how much money will you have at the end of six years? To find out the answer, turn to the table titled "Rate 15%" in Appendix C (Table C.11). Look under "Table 1" until you get to the row that is titled "Year 6." Take this factor, 2.31, and multiply it by the amount invested. The resulting figure of $134,534 is how much you will end up with (2.31 times $58,240).

Before moving on to the column marked "Table 2," take a few moments and experiment on your own with "Table 1." Make sure that you understand how it works. It is a table that can be used with any investment, growing at any rate from 5 to 20%, for any number of years from 1 to 50.

Table 2: Compounding Factor per Annum

"Table 2" is used whenever you add to an investment on a regular basis. It is the table to use whenever someone says, "I can save X amount for the next Y years." To understand better how this table works, let us assume that you can save $2,000 each year for the next

30 years. You want to know what these annual contributions will grow to, assuming that the monies are compounding at 9% annually.

Find the table marked "Rate 9%" in Appendix C (Table C.5). Look at the column marked "Table 2." Under this title, the table is described as "Growth of equal year-end deposits all growing at compound interest." Look down this column until you get to the 30-year row. That factor, 136.31, is what you will multiply your annual savings by. The answer to this multiplication problem, $272,620, is what 30 annual contributions of $2,000 each will be worth at the end of that period, assuming a 9% growth rate.

The trick to using this table is that you must use the annual amount that can be saved and use an average growth or compounding figure. Thus, if you can save $150 one month, $138 another month, and various other amounts every other month of the year, come up with an average monthly amount, such as $140 in this case. Multiply this amount by the 12 months of the year. Conversely, if you can save $3,500 during the next year, $4,500 the following year, and $4,000 the third year, come up with the average amount that can be saved annually, perhaps $4,000 in this example, and use that to figure your total amount saved.

Table 3: Sinking Fund Factor

The third column, "Table 3," is a little more difficult to use than the first two. You will use "Table 3" whenever you want to know how much will have to be saved each year to end up with a certain amount. The only possible variables here are the number of years necessary and the assumed rate of growth. Presumably, these yearly savings will be invested in *something* during the accumulation period. The best way to understand this table is to look at a couple of examples.

Let us suppose that you and your spouse want to buy a house and the necessary down payment is $40,000. The two of you have found a conservative investment that pays 8% annually. Furthermore, you figure that $4,500 can be saved each year. Anxiously, you want to know for how many years you will have to save $4,500 to end up with $40,000. We know that $4,500 multiplied by 10 equals $45,000, so working down from that we try a seven-year time horizon.

By looking under "Table 3" (staying on Table C.4, "Rate 8%") and going down until you get to the row marked "Year 7," you end up with the factor of 0.112. Divide your annual savings, $4,500, by this factor. The resulting number of $40,179 means that you need to save $4,500 for almost exactly seven years, assuming a growth rate of 8%.

Since this table is a little difficult to grasp, let us go through one more example. Assume your grandchild, age five, wants to know how much money she will have to save each year in order to end up being a millionaire by the time she reaches her mom's age, 35. You have told your granddaughter that she can get a 6% rate of return in a bank CD.

From this problem we know how much we want to end up with, $1,000,000, the amount of time involved, 30 years (when a five-year-old will become 35), and the rate of return, 6%. The only thing we do not know is how much needs to be saved each year. Turn to the table titled "Rate 6%" (Table C.2) and look under "Table 3" until you find the factor that coincides with the "Year 30" row. Take this factor, 0.013, and *multiply* $1,000,000 by it. The resulting dollar amount, $13,000, is how much will have to be saved each year.

Table 4: Discount Factor

The final subtable is easy to understand and use. This table is used whenever you want to see how long a sum of money will last, assuming a certain withdrawal rate each year. The column marked "Table 4" will also show the cumulative affects of inflation.

Let us assume that inflation will average 6% over the next decade. We want to know what the purchasing power of a dollar will be at the end of these 10 years. Turn to the table titled "Rate 6%" in Appendix C (Table C.2) and look at "Table 4," described as "How much $1 at a future date is worth today." Move down this column until you get to the row that is marked "Year 10." At the end of a decade, one dollar will be worth 56 cents (the factor of 0.558 is rounded off to 0.56).

APPENDIX C

Annuity Rate Tables

The tables that follow can be used by anyone who wants to determine what a certain sum will grow to over a specific period of time (see the column marked "Table 1"). These tables also show how much you will end up with if you invest a level amount each year, such as a $2,000 annual IRA contribution or $10,000 pension plan contribution ("Table 2"). "Table 3" indicates how much needs to be saved to reach a certain goal, such as a down payment for a house or funding a college education. Finally, "Table 4" shows the cumulative effect of what is sometimes referred to as the cruelest tax of all: inflation.

NOTE: "Factor for 1" refers to $1.00 in all tables.

Table C.1

Rate **5%**	Table 1 Compounding Factor for 1 What an initial amount becomes when growing at compound interest	Table 2 Compounding Factor For 1 Per Annum Growth of equal year-end deposits all growing at compound interest	Table 3 Sinking Fund Factor Level deposit required each year to reach 1 by a given year	Table 4 Discount Factor How much 1 at a future date is worth today
Year				
1	1.05	1.00	1.00	.952
2	1.10	2.05	.488	.907
3	1.16	3.15	.317	.864
4	1.22	4.31	.232	.823
5	1.28	5.53	.181	.784
6	1.34	6.80	.147	.746
7	1.41	8.14	.123	.711
8	1.48	9.55	.105	.677
9	1.55	11.03	.091	.645
10	1.63	12.58	.080	.614
11	1.71	14.21	.070	.585
12	1.80	15.92	.063	.557
13	1.89	17.71	.057	.530
14	1.98	19.60	.051	.505
15	2.08	21.58	.046	.481
16	2.18	23.68	.042	.458
17	2.29	25.84	.039	.436
18	2.41	28.13	.036	.416
19	2.53	30.54	.033	.396
20	2.65	33.07	.030	.377
21	2.79	35.72	.028	.359
22	2.93	38.51	.026	.342
23	3.07	41.43	.024	.326
24	3.23	44.50	.023	.310
25	3.39	47.73	.021	.295
26	3.56	51.11	.020	.281
27	3.73	54.67	.018	.268
28	3.92	58.40	.017	.255
29	4.12	62.32	.016	.243
30	4.32	66.44	.015	.231
31	4.54	70.76	.014	.220
32	4.77	75.30	.013	.210
33	5.00	80.06	.013	.200
34	5.25	85.07	.012	.190
35	5.52	90.32	.011	.181
36	5.79	95.84	.010	.173
37	6.08	101.63	.0098	.164
38	6.39	107.71	.0093	.157
39	6.71	114.10	.0088	.149
40	7.04	120.80	.0083	.142
41	7.39	127.84	.0078	.135
42	7.76	135.23	.0074	.129
43	8.15	142.99	.0070	.123
44	8.56	151.43	.0066	.117
45	8.99	159.70	.0063	.111
46	9.43	168.69	.0059	.106
47	9.91	178.12	.0056	.101
48	10.40	188.03	.0053	.096
49	10.92	198.43	.0050	.092
50	11.47	209.35	.0048	.087

Table C.2

Rate 6% Year	Table 1 Compounding Factor for 1 What an initial amount becomes when growing at compound interest	Table 2 Compounding Factor For 1 Per Annum Growth of equal year-end deposits all growing at compound interest	Table 3 Sinking Fund Factor Level deposit required each year to reach 1 by a given year	Table 4 Discount Factor How much 1 at a future date is worth today
1	1.06	1.00	1.00	.943
2	1.12	2.06	.485	.890
3	1.19	3.18	.314	.840
4	1.26	4.38	.229	.792
5	1.34	5.64	.177	.747
6	1.42	6.98	.143	.705
7	1.50	8.39	.119	.665
8	1.59	9.90	.101	.627
9	1.69	11.49	.087	.592
10	1.80	13.18	.076	.558
11	1.90	14.97	.067	.527
12	2.01	16.87	.059	.497
13	2.13	18.88	.053	.469
14	2.26	21.02	.048	.442
15	2.40	23.28	.043	.417
16	2.54	25.67	.039	.394
17	2.69	28.21	.036	.371
18	2.85	30.91	.032	.350
19	3.03	33.76	.030	.331
20	3.21	36.79	.027	.312
21	3.40	39.99	.025	.294
22	3.60	43.39	.023	.278
23	3.82	47.00	.021	.262
24	4.05	50.82	.020	.247
25	4.29	54.86	.018	.233
26	4.55	59.16	.017	.220
27	4.82	63.71	.016	.207
28	5.11	68.53	.015	.196
29	5.42	73.64	.014	.185
30	5.74	79.06	.013	.174
31	6.09	84.80	.012	.164
32	6.45	90.89	.011	.155
33	6.84	97.34	.010	.146
34	7.25	104.18	.0096	.138
35	7.69	111.43	.0090	.130
36	8.15	119.12	.0084	.123
37	8.64	127.27	.0079	.116
38	9.14	135.90	.0074	.109
39	9.70	145.06	.0069	.103
40	10.29	154.76	.0065	.097
41	10.90	165.05	.0061	.092
42	11.56	175.95	.0057	.087
43	12.25	187.51	.0053	.082
44	12.99	199.76	.0050	.077
45	13.77	212.74	.0047	.073
46	14.59	226.51	.0044	.069
47	15.47	241.10	.0042	.065
48	16.39	256.56	.0039	.061
49	17.38	272.96	.0037	.058
50	18.42	290.34	.0034	.054

Table C.3

Rate 7% Year	Table 1 Compounding Factor for 1 What an initial amount becomes when growing at compound interest	Table 2 Compounding Factor For 1 Per Annum Growth of equal year-end deposits all growing at compound interest	Table 3 Sinking Fund Factor Level deposit required each year to reach 1 by a given year	Table 4 Discount Factor How much 1 at a future date is worth today
1	1.07	1.00	1.00	.935
2	1.15	2.07	.483	.873
3	1.23	3.22	.311	.816
4	1.31	4.44	.225	.763
5	1.40	5.75	.174	.713
6	1.50	7.15	.140	.666
7	1.61	8.65	.116	.623
8	1.72	10.26	.098	.582
9	1.84	11.98	.084	.544
10	1.97	13.82	.072	.508
11	2.11	15.78	.063	.475
12	2.25	17.89	.056	.444
13	2.41	20.14	.050	.415
14	2.58	22.55	.044	.388
15	2.76	25.13	.040	.363
16	2.95	27.89	.036	.339
17	3.16	30.84	.032	.317
18	3.38	34.00	.029	.296
19	3.62	37.38	.027	.277
20	3.87	41.00	.024	.258
21	4.14	44.87	.022	.242
22	4.43	49.01	.020	.226
23	4.74	53.44	.019	.211
24	5.07	58.18	.017	.197
25	5.43	63.25	.016	.184
26	5.81	68.68	.015	.172
27	6.21	74.48	.013	.161
28	6.65	80.70	.012	.150
29	7.11	87.35	.012	.141
30	7.61	94.46	.011	.131
31	8.15	102.07	.0098	.123
32	8.72	110.22	.0091	.115
33	9.33	118.93	.0084	.107
34	9.98	128.26	.0078	.100
35	10.68	138.24	.0072	.094
36	11.42	148.91	.0067	.088
37	12.22	160.34	.0062	.082
38	13.08	172.56	.0058	.077
39	14.00	185.64	.0054	.072
40	14.98	199.64	.0050	.067
41	16.02	214.61	.0047	.062
42	17.14	230.63	.0043	.058
43	18.34	247.78	.0040	.055
44	19.63	266.12	.0038	.051
45	21.00	285.75	.0035	.048
46	22.47	306.75	.0033	.045
47	24.05	329.22	.0030	.042
48	25.73	353.27	.0028	.039
49	27.53	379.00	.0026	.036
50	29.46	406.53	.0025	.034

Table C.4

Rate 8% Year	Table 1 Compounding Factor for 1 What an initial amount becomes when growing at compound interest	Table 2 Compounding Factor For 1 Per Annum Growth of equal year-end deposits all growing at compound interest	Table 3 Sinking Fund Factor Level deposit required each year to reach 1 by a given year	Table 4 Discount Factor How much 1 at a future date is worth today
1	1.08	1.00	1.00	.926
2	1.17	2.08	.481	.857
3	1.26	3.25	.308	.794
4	1.36	4.51	.222	.735
5	1.47	5.87	.171	.681
6	1.59	7.34	.136	.630
7	1.71	8.92	.112	.585
8	1.85	10.64	.094	.540
9	2.00	12.49	.080	.500
10	2.16	14.49	.069	.463
11	2.33	16.65	.060	.429
12	2.52	18.98	.053	.397
13	2.72	21.50	.047	.368
14	2.94	24.21	.041	.341
15	3.17	27.15	.037	.315
16	3.43	30.32	.033	.292
17	3.70	33.75	.030	.270
18	4.00	37.45	.027	.250
19	4.32	41.45	.024	.232
20	4.66	45.76	.022	.215
21	5.03	50.42	.020	.199
22	5.44	55.46	.018	.184
23	5.87	60.89	.016	.170
24	6.34	66.77	.015	.158
25	6.85	73.11	.014	.146
26	7.40	79.95	.013	.135
27	7.99	87.35	.012	.125
28	8.63	95.34	.011	.116
29	9.32	103.97	.0096	.107
30	10.06	113.28	.0088	.099
31	10.87	123.35	.0081	.092
32	11.74	134.21	.0075	.085
33	12.68	145.95	.0069	.079
34	13.69	158.63	.0063	.073
35	14.79	172.32	.0058	.068
36	15.97	187.10	.0054	.063
37	17.25	203.07	.0049	.058
38	18.63	220.32	.0045	.054
39	20.12	238.94	.0042	.050
40	21.73	259.06	.0039	.046
41	23.46	280.78	.0036	.043
42	25.34	304.24	.0033	.040
43	27.37	329.58	.0030	.037
44	29.56	356.95	.0028	.034
45	31.92	386.51	.0026	.031
46	34.74	418.43	.0024	.029
47	37.23	452.90	.0022	.027
48	40.21	490.13	.0020	.025
49	43.43	530.34	.0019	.023
50	46.90	573.77	.0017	.021

Table C.5

Rate 9% Year	Table 1 Compounding Factor for 1 What an initial amount becomes when growing at compound interest	Table 2 Compounding Factor For 1 Per Annum Growth of equal year-end deposits all growing at compound interest	Table 3 Sinking Fund Factor Level deposit required each year to reach 1 by a given year	Table 4 Discount Factor How much 1 at a future date is worth today
1	1.09	1.00	1.00	.917
2	1.19	2.09	.479	.842
3	1.30	3.28	.305	.772
4	1.41	4.57	.219	.708
5	1.54	5.99	.167	.650
6	1.68	7.52	.133	.596
7	1.83	9.20	.109	.547
8	2.00	11.03	.091	.502
9	2.17	13.02	.077	.460
10	2.37	15.19	.066	.422
11	2.58	17.56	.057	.388
12	2.81	20.14	.050	.356
13	3.07	22.95	.044	.326
14	3.34	26.02	.038	.299
15	3.64	29.36	.034	.275
16	3.97	33.00	.030	.252
17	4.33	36.97	.027	.231
18	4.72	41.30	.024	.212
19	5.14	46.02	.022	.195
20	5.60	51.16	.020	.178
21	6.11	56.77	.018	.164
22	6.66	62.87	.016	.150
23	7.26	69.53	.014	.138
24	7.91	76.79	.013	.126
25	8.62	84.70	.012	.116
26	9.40	93.32	.011	.106
27	10.25	102.72	.0098	.098
28	11.17	112.97	.0089	.090
29	12.17	124.14	.0081	.082
30	13.27	136.31	.0073	.075
31	14.46	149.58	.0067	.069
32	15.76	164.04	.0061	.063
33	17.18	179.80	.0056	.058
34	18.73	196.98	.0051	.053
35	20.41	215.71	.0046	.049
36	22.25	236.12	.0042	.045
37	24.25	258.38	.0039	.041
38	26.44	282.63	.0035	.038
39	28.82	309.07	.0032	.035
40	31.41	337.88	.0030	.032
41	34.24	369.29	.0027	.029
42	37.32	403.53	.0025	.027
43	40.68	440.85	.0023	.025
44	44.34	481.52	.0021	.023
45	48.33	525.86	.0019	.021
46	52.68	574.19	.0017	.019
47	57.42	626.86	.0016	.017
48	62.59	684.28	.0015	.016
49	68.22	746.87	.0013	.015
50	74.36	815.08	.0012	.014

Table C.6

Rate 10%	Table 1 Compounding Factor for 1 What an initial amount becomes when growing at compound interest	Table 2 Compounding Factor For 1 Per Annum Growth of equal year-end deposits all growing at compound interest	Table 3 Sinking Fund Factor Level deposit required each year to reach 1 by a given year	Table 4 Discount Factor How much 1 at a future date is worth today
Year				
1	1.10	1.00	1.00	.909
2	1.21	2.10	.476	.827
3	1.33	3.31	.302	.751
4	1.46	4.64	.216	.683
5	1.61	6.11	.164	.621
6	1.77	7.72	.130	.565
7	1.95	9.49	.105	.513
8	2.14	11.44	.087	.467
9	2.36	13.58	.074	.424
10	2.59	15.94	.063	.386
11	2.85	18.53	.054	.351
12	3.14	21.38	.047	.319
13	3.45	24.52	.041	.290
14	3.80	27.97	.036	.263
15	4.18	31.77	.032	.239
16	4.60	35.95	.028	.218
17	5.06	40.55	.025	.198
18	5.56	45.60	.022	.180
19	6.12	51.16	.020	.164
20	6.73	57.28	.018	.149
21	7.40	64.00	.016	.135
22	8.14	71.40	.014	.123
23	8.95	79.50	.013	.112
24	9.85	88.50	.011	.102
25	10.84	98.35	.010	.092
26	11.92	109.18	.0091	.084
27	13.11	121.10	.0083	.076
28	14.42	134.21	.0075	.069
29	15.86	148.63	.0067	.063
30	17.45	164.49	.0061	.057
31	19.19	181.94	.0055	.052
32	21.11	201.14	.0050	.047
33	23.23	222.25	.0045	.043
34	25.55	245.48	.0040	.039
35	28.10	271.02	.0037	.036
36	30.91	299.13	.0033	.032
37	34.00	330.04	.0030	.029
38	37.40	364.04	.0028	.027
39	41.15	401.45	.0025	.024
40	45.26	442.59	.0023	.022
41	49.79	487.85	.0021	.020
42	54.76	537.64	.0019	.018
43	60.24	592.40	.0017	.017
44	66.26	652.64	.0015	.015
45	72.89	718.91	.0014	.014
46	80.18	791.80	.0013	.013
47	88.20	871.95	.0012	.011
48	97..01	960.17	.0010	.010
49	106.72	1,057.19	.0009	.0093
50	117.39	1,163.91	.0009	.0085

Table C.7

Rate 11%	Table 1 Compounding Factor for 1 What an initial amount becomes when growing at compound interest	Table 2 Compounding Factor For 1 Per Annum Growth of equal year-end deposits all growing at compound interest	Table 3 Sinking Fund Factor Level deposit required each year to reach 1 by a given year	Table 4 Discount Factor How much 1 at a future date is worth today
Year				
1	1.11	1.00	1.00	.901
2	1.23	2.11	.474	.812
3	1.37	3.34	.299	.731
4	1.52	4.71	.212	.659
5	1.69	6.23	.161	.594
6	1.87	7.91	.126	.535
7	2.08	9.78	.102	.482
8	2.31	11.86	.084	.434
9	2.56	14.16	.071	.391
10	2.84	16.72	.060	.352
11	3.15	19.56	.051	.317
12	3.50	22.71	.044	.286
13	3.88	26.21	.038	.258
14	4.31	30.10	.033	.232
15	4.79	34.41	.029	.209
16	5.31	39.19	.026	.188
17	5.90	44.50	.023	.170
18	6.54	50.40	.020	.153
19	7.26	56.94	.018	.138
20	8.06	64.20	.016	.124
21	8.95	72.27	.014	.112
22	9.93	81.21	.012	.101
23	11.03	91.15	.011	.091
24	12.24	102.17	.0098	.082
25	13.59	114.41	.0087	.074
26	15.08	128.00	.0078	.066
27	16.74	143.08	.0070	.060
28	18.58	159.82	.0062	.054
29	20.62	178.40	.0056	.049
30	22.89	199.02	.0050	.044
31	25.41	221.91	.0045	.039
32	28.21	247.32	.0040	.036
33	31.31	275.53	.0036	.032
34	34.75	306.84	.0032	.029
35	38.58	341.59	.0029	.026
36	42.82	380.16	.0026	.023
37	47.53	422.98	.0024	.021
38	52.76	470.51	.0021	.019
39	58.56	523.27	.0019	.017
40	65.00	581.83	.0017	.015
41	72.15	646.83	.0016	.014
42	80.09	718.98	.0014	.013
43	88.90	799.07	.0013	.011
44	98.68	887.96	.0011	.010
45	109.53	986.64	.0010	.0091
46	121.58	1,096.17	.0009	.0082
47	134.95	1,217.75	.0008	.0074
48	149.80	1,352.70	.0007	.0067
49	166.28	1,502.50	.0007	.0060
50	184.57	1,668.77	.0006	.0054

Table C.8

Rate 12%	Table 1 Compounding Factor for 1 What an initial amount becomes when growing at compound interest	Table 2 Compounding Factor For 1 Per Annum Growth of equal year-end deposits all growing at compound interest	Table 3 Sinking Fund Factor Level deposit required each year to reach 1 by a given year	Table 4 Discount Factor How much 1 at a future date is worth today
Year				
1	1.12	1.00	1.00	.893
2	1.25	2.12	.472	.797
3	1.41	3.37	.296	.712
4	1.57	4.78	.209	.636
5	1.76	6.35	.157	.567
6	1.97	8.12	.123	.507
7	2.21	10.09	.099	.452
8	2.48	12.30	.081	.404
9	2.77	14.78	.068	.361
10	3.11	17.55	.057	.322
11	3.48	20.66	.048	.288
12	3.90	24.13	.041	.257
13	4.36	28.03	.036	.229
14	4.89	32.39	.031	.205
15	5.47	37.30	.027	.183
16	6.13	42.75	.023	.163
17	6.87	48.88	.021	.146
18	7.69	55.75	.018	.130
19	8.61	63.44	.016	.116
20	9.65	72.05	.014	.104
21	10.80	81.70	.012	.093
22	12.10	92.50	.011	.083
23	13.55	104.60	.0096	.074
24	15.18	118.16	.0085	.066
25	17.00	133.33	.0075	.059
26	19.04	150.33	.0067	.053
27	21.32	169.37	.0059	.047
28	23.88	190.70	.0052	.042
29	26.75	214.58	.0047	.037
30	29.96	241.33	.0041	.033
31	33.56	271.29	.0037	.030
32	37.58	304.85	.0033	.027
33	42.09	342.43	.0029	.024
34	47.14	384.52	.0026	.021
35	52.80	431.66	.0023	.019
36	59.14	484.46	.0021	.017
37	66.23	543.60	.0028	.015
38	74.18	609.83	.0026	.014
39	83.08	684.01	.0015	.012
40	93.05	767.09	.0013	.011
41	104.22	860.14	.0012	.0096
42	116.72	964.36	.0010	.0086
43	130.73	1,081.08	.0009	.0077
44	146.42	1,211.81	.0008	.0068
45	163.99	1,358.23	.0007	.0061
46	183.67	1,522.22	.0007	.0055
47	205.71	1,705.88	.0006	.0049
48	230.39	1,911.59	.0005	.0043
49	258.04	2,141.98	.0005	.0039
50	289.00	2,400.02	.0004	.0035

Table C.9

Rate 13% Year	Table 1 Compounding Factor for 1 What an initial amount becomes when growing at compound interest	Table 2 Compounding Factor For 1 Per Annum Growth of equal year-end deposits all growing at compound interest	Table 3 Sinking Fund Factor Level deposit required each year to reach 1 by a given year	Table 4 Discount Factor How much 1 at a future date is worth today
1	1.13	1.00	1.00	.885
2	1.28	2.13	.470	.783
3	1.44	3.41	.294	.693
4	1.63	4.85	.206	.613
5	1.84	6.48	.154	.543
6	2.08	8.32	.120	.480
7	2.35	10.41	.096	.425
8	2.66	12.76	.078	.376
9	3.00	15.42	.065	.333
10	3.40	18.42	.054	.295
11	3.84	21.81	.046	.261
12	4.34	25.65	.039	.231
13	4.90	29.99	.033	.204
14	5.54	34.88	.029	.181
15	6.25	40.42	.025	.160
16	7.07	46.67	.021	.142
17	7.99	53.74	.019	.125
18	9.02	61.73	.016	.111
19	10.20	70.75	.014	.098
20	11.52	80.95	.012	.087
21	13.02	92.47	.011	.077
22	14.71	105.49	.0095	.068
23	16.63	120.20	.0083	.060
24	18.79	136.83	.0073	.053
25	21.23	155.62	.0064	.047
26	23.99	176.85	.0057	.042
27	27.11	200.84	.0050	.037
28	30.63	227.95	.0044	.033
29	34.62	258.58	.0039	.029
30	39.12	293.20	.0034	.026
31	44.20	332.32	.0030	.023
32	49.95	376.52	.0027	.020
33	56.44	426.46	.0024	.018
34	63.78	482.90	.0021	.016
35	72.07	546.68	.0018	.014
36	81.44	618.75	.0016	.012
37	92.02	700.19	.0014	.011
38	103.99	792.21	.0013	.0096
39	117.51	896.20	.0011	.0085
40	132.78	1,013.70	.0010	.0075
41	150.04	1,146.49	.0009	.0067
42	169.55	1,296.53	.0008	.0059
43	191.59	1,455.08	.0007	.0052
44	216.50	1,657.67	.0006	.0046
45	244.64	1,874.17	.0005	.0041
46	276.45	2,118.81	.0005	.0036
47	312.38	2,395.25	.0004	.0032
48	352.99	2,707.63	.0004	.0028
49	398.88	3,060.63	.0003	.0025
50	450.74	3,459.51	.0003	.0022

Table C.10

Rate 14%	Table 1 Compounding Factor for 1 What an initial amount becomes when growing at compound interest	Table 2 Compounding Factor For 1 Per Annum Growth of equal year-end deposits all growing at compound interest	Table 3 Sinking Fund Factor Level deposit required each year to reach 1 by a given year	Table 4 Discount Factor How much 1 at a future date is worth today
Year				
1	1.14	1.00	1.00	.877
2	1.30	2.14	.467	.770
3	1.48	3.44	.291	.675
4	1.69	4.92	.203	.592
5	1.93	6.61	.151	.519
6	2.20	8.54	.117	.456
7	2.50	10.73	.093	.400
8	2.85	13.23	.076	.351
9	3.25	16.09	.062	.308
10	3.71	19.34	.052	.270
11	4.23	23.05	.043	.237
12	4.82	27.27	.037	.208
13	5.49	32.09	.031	.182
14	6.26	37.58	.027	.160
15	7.14	43.84	.023	.141
16	8.14	50.98	.020	.123
17	9.28	59.12	.017	.108
18	10.58	68.39	.015	.095
19	12.06	78.97	.013	.083
20	13.74	91.03	.011	.073
21	15.67	104.77	.0096	.064
22	17.86	120.44	.0083	.056
23	20.36	138.30	.0072	.049
24	23.21	158.66	.0063	.043
25	26.46	181.87	.0055	.038
26	30.17	208.33	.0048	.033
27	34.39	238.50	.0042	.029
28	39.21	272.89	.0037	.026
29	44.69	312.09	.0032	.022
30	50.95	356.79	.0028	.020
31	58.08	407.74	.0025	.017
32	66.22	465.82	.0022	.015
33	75.49	532.04	.0019	.013
34	86.05	607.52	.0017	.012
35	98.10	693.57	.0014	.010
36	111.83	791.67	.0013	.0089
37	127.49	903.51	.0011	.0078
38	145.34	1,031.00	.0010	.0069
39	165.69	1,176.34	.0009	.0060
40	188.88	1,342.03	.0008	.0053
41	215.34	1,530.91	.0007	.0046
42	245.47	1,746.24	.0006	.0041
43	279.84	1,991.71	.0005	.0036
44	319.02	2,271.55	.0004	.0031
45	363.68	2,590.57	.0004	.0028
46	414.59	2,954.24	.0003	.0024
47	472.64	3,368.84	.0003	.0021
48	538.81	3,841.48	.0003	.0019
49	614.24	4,380.28	.0002	.0016
50	700.23	4,994.52	.0002	.0014

Table C.11

Rate 15% Year	Table 1 Compounding Factor for 1 What an initial amount becomes when growing at compound interest	Table 2 Compounding Factor For 1 Per Annum Growth of equal year-end deposits all growing at compound interest	Table 3 Sinking Fund Factor Level deposit required each year to reach 1 by a given year	Table 4 Discount Factor How much 1 at a future date is worth today
1	1.15	1.00	1.00	.870
2	1.32	2.15	.465	.756
3	1.52	3.47	.288	.658
4	1.75	4.99	.200	.572
5	2.01	6.74	.148	.497
6	2.31	8.75	.114	.432
7	2.66	11.07	.090	.376
8	3.06	13.73	.073	.327
9	3.52	16.79	.060	.284
10	4.05	20.30	.049	.247
11	4.65	24.35	.041	.215
12	5.35	29.00	.035	.187
13	6.15	34.51	.029	.163
14	7.08	40.51	.025	.141
15	8.14	47.58	.021	.123
16	9.36	55.72	.018	.107
17	10.76	65.08	.015	.093
18	12.38	75.84	.013	.081
19	14.23	88.21	.011	.070
20	16.37	102.44	.010	.061
21	18.82	118.81	.0084	.053
22	21.65	137.63	.0073	.046
23	24.89	159.28	.0063	.040
24	28.63	184.17	.0054	.035
25	32.92	212.79	.0047	.030
26	37.86	245.71	.0040	.026
27	43.54	283.57	.0035	.023
28	50.07	327.10	.0030	.020
29	57.58	377.17	.0027	.017
30	66.21	434.75	.0023	.015
31	76.14	500.96	.0020	.013
32	87.57	577.10	.0017	.011
33	100.70	664.67	.0015	.0099
34	115.81	765.37	.0013	.0086
35	133.18	881.17	.0011	.0075
36	153.15	1,014.35	.0010	.0065
37	176.12	1,167.50	.0009	.0057
38	202.54	1,343.62	.0008	.0049
39	232.92	1,546.17	.0007	.0043
40	267.86	1,779.09	.0006	.0037
41	308.04	2,046.95	.0005	.0033
42	354.25	2,355.00	.0004	.0028
43	407.39	2,709.25	.0004	.0025
44	468.50	3,116.63	.0003	.0021
45	538.77	3,585.13	.0003	.0019
46	619.58	4,123.90	.0002	.0016
47	712.52	4,743.48	.0002	.0014
48	819.40	5,456.01	.0002	.0012
49	942.31	6,275.41	.0002	.0011
50	1,083.66	7,217.72	.0001	.0010

Table C.12

Rate 16%	Table 1 Compounding Factor for 1 What an initial amount becomes when growing at compound interest	Table 2 Compounding Factor For 1 Per Annum Growth of equal year-end deposits all growing at compound interest	Table 3 Sinking Fund Factor Level deposit required each year to reach 1 by a given year	Table 4 Discount Factor How much 1 at a future date is worth today
Year				
1	1.16	1.00	1.00	.862
2	1.35	2.16	.463	.743
3	1.56	3.51	.285	.641
4	1.81	5.07	.197	.552
5	2.10	6.88	.145	.476
6	2.44	8.98	.111	.410
7	2.83	11.41	.088	.354
8	3.28	14.24	.070	.305
9	3.80	17.52	.057	.263
10	4.41	21.32	.047	.227
11	5.12	25.73	.039	.195
12	5.94	30.85	.032	.169
13	6.89	36.79	.027	.145
14	7.99	43.67	.023	.125
15	9.27	51.66	.019	.108
16	10.75	60.93	.016	.093
17	12.47	71.67	.014	.080
18	14.46	84.10	.012	.069
19	16.78	98.60	.010	.060
20	19.46	115.38	.0087	.051
21	22.57	134.84	.0074	.044
22	26.19	157.42	.0064	.038
23	30.38	183.60	.0055	.033
24	35.24	213.98	.0047	.028
25	40.87	249.21	.0040	.025
26	47.41	290.09	.0035	.021
27	55.00	337.50	.0030	.018
28	63.80	392.50	.0026	.016
29	74.01	456.30	.0022	.014
30	85.85	530.31	.0019	.012
31	99.59	616.16	.0016	.010
32	115.52	715.75	.0014	.0087
33	134.00	831.27	.0012	.0075
34	155.44	965.29	.0010	.0064
35	180.31	1,120.71	.0009	.0056
36	209.16	1,301.03	.0008	.0047
37	242.63	1,510.19	.0007	.0041
38	281.45	1,752.82	.0006	.0036
39	326.48	2,034.27	.0005	.0031
40	378.72	2,360.76	.0004	.0026
41	439.32	2,739.48	.0004	.0023
42	509.61	3,178.80	.0003	.0020
43	591.14	3,688.40	.0003	.0017
44	685.73	4,279.55	.0002	.0015
45	795.44	4,965.27	.0002	.0013
46	922.71	5,760.72	.0002	.0011
47	1,070.35	6,683.43	.0002	.0009
48	1,241.61	7,753.78	.0001	.0008
49	1,440.26	8,995.39	.0001	.0007
50	1,670.70	10,435.65	.0001	.0006

Table C.13

Rate 17% Year	Table 1 Compounding Factor for 1 What an initial amount becomes when growing at compound interest	Table 2 Compounding Factor For 1 Per Annum Growth of equal year-end deposits all growing at compound interest	Table 3 Sinking Fund Factor Level deposit required each year to reach 1 by a given year	Table 4 Discount Factor How much 1 at a future date is worth today
1	1.17	1.00	1.00	.855
2	1.37	2.17	.461	.731
3	1.60	3.54	.283	.624
4	1.87	5.14	.195	.534
5	2.19	7.01	.143	.456
6	2.57	9.21	.109	.390
7	3.00	11.77	.085	.333
8	3.51	14.77	.068	.285
9	4.11	18.29	.055	.243
10	4.81	22.39	.045	.208
11	5.62	27.20	.037	.178
12	6.58	32.82	.031	.152
13	7.70	39.40	.025	.130
14	9.01	47.10	.021	.111
15	10.54	56.11	.018	.095
16	12.33	66.65	.015	.081
17	14.43	79.98	.013	.069
18	16.88	93.41	.011	.059
19	19.75	110.29	.0091	.051
20	23.11	130.03	.0077	.043
21	27.03	153.14	.0065	.037
22	31.63	180.17	.0056	.032
23	37.01	211.80	.0047	.027
24	43.30	248.81	.0040	.023
25	50.66	292.11	.0034	.020
26	59.27	342.76	.0029	.017
27	69.35	402.03	.0025	.014
28	81.13	471.38	.0021	.012
29	94.93	552.51	.0018	.011
30	111.06	647.44	.0016	.0090
31	129.95	758.50	.0013	.0077
32	152.04	888.45	.0011	.0066
33	177.88	1,040.49	.0010	.0056
34	208.12	1,218.37	.0008	.0048
35	243.50	1,426.49	.0007	.0041
36	284.90	1,670.00	.0006	.0035
37	333.33	1,954.89	.0005	.0030
38	390.00	2,288.23	.0004	.0026
39	456.30	2,678.22	.00037	.0022
40	533.87	3,134.52	.00032	.0019
41	624.63	3,668.39	.00027	.0016
42	730.81	4,293.02	.00023	.0014
43	855.05	5,023.83	.00020	.0012
44	1,000.41	5,878.88	.00017	.0010
45	1,170.48	6,879.29	.00015	.00085
46	1,369.46	8,049.77	.00012	.00073
47	1,602.27	9,419.23	.00011	.00062
48	1,874.66	11,021.50	.00010	.00053
49	2,193.35	12,896.16	.00008	.00046
50	2,566.22	15,089.50	.00006	.00039

Table C.14

Rate 18%	Table 1 Compounding Factor for 1 What an initial amount becomes when growing at compound interest	Table 2 Compounding Factor For 1 Per Annum Growth of equal year-end deposits all growing at compound interest	Table 3 Sinking Fund Factor Level deposit required each year to reach 1 by a given year	Table 4 Discount Factor How much 1 at a future date is worth today
Year				
1	1.18	1.00	1.00	.848
2	1.39	2.18	.459	.718
3	1.64	3.57	.280	.609
4	1.94	5.22	.192	.516
5	2.29	7.15	.140	.437
6	2.70	9.44	.106	.370
7	3.19	12.14	.082	.314
8	3.76	15.33	.065	.266
9	4.44	19.09	.052	.226
10	5.23	23.52	.043	.191
11	6.18	28.76	.035	.162
12	7.29	34.93	.029	.137
13	8.60	42.22	.024	.116
14	10.15	50.82	.020	.099
15	11.97	60.97	.016	.084
16	14.13	72.94	.014	.071
17	16.67	87.07	.012	.060
18	19.67	103.74	.010	.051
19	23.21	123.41	.0081	.043
20	27.39	146.63	.0068	.037
21	32.32	174.02	.0058	.031
22	38.14	206.34	.0049	.026
23	45.01	244.49	.0041	.022
24	53.11	289.50	.0035	.019
25	62.67	342.60	.0029	.016
26	73.95	405.27	.0025	.014
27	87.26	479.22	.0021	.012
28	102.97	566.48	.0018	.0097
29	121.50	669.45	.0015	.0082
30	143.37	790.95	.0013	.0070
31	169.18	934.32	.0011	.0059
32	199.63	1,103.50	.00091	.0050
33	235.56	1,303.13	.00077	.0042
34	277.96	1,538.69	.00065	.0036
35	328.00	1,816.65	.00055	.0031
36	387.04	2,144.65	.00047	.0026
37	456.70	2,531.69	.00040	.0022
38	538.91	2,988.39	.00034	.0019
39	635.91	3,527.30	.00028	.0016
40	750.38	4,163.21	.00024	.0013
41	885.45	4,913.59	.00020	.0011
42	1,044.83	5,799.04	.00017	.00096
43	1,232.90	6,843.87	.00015	.00081
44	1,454.82	8,076.76	.00012	.00069
45	1,716.68	9,531.58	.00011	.00058
46	2,025.69	11,248.26	.00009	.00049
47	2,390.31	13,273.95	.00008	.00042
48	2,820.57	15,664.26	.00006	.00036
49	3,328.27	18,484.83	.00005	.00030
50	3,927.36	21,813.09	.00004	.00026

Table C.15

Rate 19%	Table 1 Compounding Factor for 1 What an initial amount becomes when growing at compound interest	Table 2 Compounding Factor For 1 Per Annum Growth of equal year-end deposits all growing at compound interest	Table 3 Sinking Fund Factor Level deposit required each year to reach 1 by a given year	Table 4 Discount Factor How much 1 at a future date is worth today
Year				
1	1.19	1.00	1.00	.840
2	1.42	2.19	.457	.706
3	1.69	3.61	.277	.593
4	2.01	5.29	.189	.499
5	2.39	7.30	.137	.419
6	2.84	9.68	.103	.352
7	3.38	12.52	.080	.296
8	4.02	15.90	.063	.249
9	4.79	19.92	.050	.209
10	5.69	24.71	.041	.176
11	6.78	30.40	.033	.148
12	8.06	37.18	.027	.124
13	9.60	45.24	.022	.104
14	11.42	54.84	.018	.088
15	13.59	66.26	.015	.074
16	16.17	79.85	.013	.062
17	19.24	96.02	.010	.052
18	22.90	115.27	.0087	.044
19	27.25	138.17	.0072	.037
20	32.43	165.42	.0061	.031
21	38.59	197.85	.0051	.026
22	45.92	236.44	.0042	.022
23	54.65	282.36	.0035	.018
24	65.03	337.01	.0030	.014
25	77.39	402.04	.0025	.013
26	92.09	479.43	.0021	.011
27	109.59	571.52	.0018	.0091
28	130.41	681.11	.0015	.0077
29	155.19	811.52	.0012	.0064
30	184.68	966.71	.0010	.0054
31	219.76	1,151.39	.00087	.0046
32	261.52	1,371.15	.00073	.0038
33	311.21	1,632.67	.00061	.0032
34	370.34	1,943.88	.00051	.0027
35	440.70	2,314.21	.00043	.0023
36	524.43	2,754.91	.00036	.0019
37	624.08	3,279.35	.00031	.0016
38	742.65	3,903.42	.00026	.0014
39	883.75	4,646.07	.00022	.0011
40	1,051.67	5,529.83	.00018	.00095
41	1,251.48	6,581.50	.00015	.00080
42	1,489.27	7,832.98	.00013	.00067
43	1,772.23	9,322.25	.00011	.00056
44	2,108.95	11,094.47	.00009	.00047
45	2,509.65	13,203.42	.00008	.00040
46	2,986.48	15,713.08	.00006	.00034
47	3,553.92	18,699.56	.00005	.00028
48	4,229.16	22,253.48	.00005	.00024
49	5,032.70	26,482.64	.00004	.00020
50	5,988.91	31,515.34	.00003	.00017

Table C.16

Rate 20%	Table 1 Compounding Factor for 1 What an initial amount becomes when growing at compound interest	Table 2 Compounding Factor For 1 Per Annum Growth of equal year-end deposits all growing at compound interest	Table 3 Sinking Fund Factor Level deposit required each year to reach 1 by a given year	Table 4 Discount Factor How much 1 at a future date is worth today
Year				
1	1.20	1.00	1.00	.833
2	1.44	2.20	.455	.694
3	1.73	3.64	.275	.579
4	2.07	5.37	.186	.482
5	2.49	7.44	.134	.402
6	2.99	9.93	.101	.335
7	3.58	12.92	.077	.279
8	4.30	16.50	.061	.233
9	5.16	20.80	.048	.194
10	6.19	25.96	.039	.162
11	7.43	32.15	.031	.135
12	8.92	39.58	.025	.112
13	10.70	48.50	.021	.094
14	12.84	59.20	.017	.078
15	15.41	72.04	.014	.065
16	18.49	87.44	.011	.054
17	22.19	105.93	.0094	.045
18	26.62	128.12	.0078	.038
19	31.95	154.74	.0065	.031
20	38.34	186.69	.0054	.026
21	46.01	225.03	.0044	.022
22	55.21	271.03	.0037	.018
23	66.25	326.24	.0031	.015
24	79.50	392.48	.0026	.013
25	95.40	471.98	.0021	.010
26	114.48	567.38	.0018	.0087
27	137.37	681.85	.0015	.0073
28	164.84	819.22	.0012	.0061
29	197.81	984.07	.0010	.0051
30	237.38	1,181.88	.00085	.0042
31	284.85	1,419.26	.00071	.0035
32	341.82	1,704.11	.00059	.0029
33	410.19	2,045.93	.00049	.0024
34	492.22	2,456.12	.00041	.0020
35	590.67	2,948.34	.00034	.0017
36	708.80	3,539.01	.00028	.0014
37	850.56	4,247.81	.00024	.0012
38	1,020.68	5,098.37	.00020	.00098
39	1,224.81	6,119.05	.00016	.00082
40	1,469.77	7,343.86	.00014	.00068
41	1,763.73	8,813.63	.00011	.00057
42	2,116.47	10,577.36	.00010	.00047
43	2,539.77	12,693.83	.00008	.00039
44	3,047.72	15,233.59	.00007	.00033
45	3,657.26	18,281.31	.00006	.00027
46	4,388.71	21,938.57	.00005	.00023
47	5,266.46	26,327.29	.00004	.00019
48	6,319.75	31,593.74	.00003	.00016
49	7,583.70	37,913.49	.00003	.00013
50	9,100.44	45,497.19	.00002	.00011

APPENDIX D

Survivorship Tables

The charts in this appendix indicate what happens under a wide range of circumstances, including what is referred to as a *case*. By first looking for the case that applies, you can see what happens to the annuity contract shown and whether or not a taxable event is triggered.

These are illustrations of various ownership, annuitant, and beneficiary designations and the federal income, estate, and gift tax consequences of each *at the time of the first death*.

Note: If a contingent owner has been named rather than a joint owner, and the nonannuitant owner dies, the cash surrender value is payable to the contingent owner. Should the contingent owner be the surviving spouse, he or she may assume ownership of the contract. In the case of joint owners, it is assumed that each owner contributed one half of the annuity premiums to the contract.

Table D.1 *Survivorship cases 1—5*

Tax Implications Chart for Nonqualified Annuity Contracts

Case	Owner	Joint Owner	Annuitant	Beneficiary	First Death
1	Husband	None	Husband	Wife	Husband*
2	Husband	None	Husband	Wife	Wife
3	Husband	None	Husband	Child	Husband*
4	Husband	None	Wife	Husband	Husband
5	Husband	None	Wife	Husband	Wife*

Case	Contract Disposition	Can Contract Continue?	1099 Issued?
1	Wife may continue contract in deferred status with herself as owner or elect lump sum or annuity option. Full contract value is payable.	Yes	No, if wife continues contract.
2	Contract remains intact. New beneficiary named.	Yes	No
3	Child must elect lump sum or annuity option. Full contract value is payable.	No	Yes
4	Wife may continue contract in deferred status with herself as owner or elect lump sum or annuity option. Cash surrender value is payable.	Yes	No, if wife continues contract.
5	Husband may continue contract in deferred status or elect lump sum or annuity option. Full contract value is payable.	Yes	No, if husband continues contract.

Case	Federal Income Tax	Federal Estate Tax	Federal Gift Tax
1	All deferred income taxed to wife at time actually paid out of annuity contract.	Full contract value included in husband's estate - marital deduction available.	None
2	None	None	None
3	All deferred income taxable to child at time actually paid out of contract.	Full contract value included in husband's estate.	None
4	All deferred income taxed to wife at time actually paid out of contract.	Full contract value included in husband's estate - marital deduction available.	None
5	All deferred income taxed to husband at time actually paid out of annuity contract.	None	None

*Minimum death benefit provision applies upon death of the annuitant.

Table D.2 *Survivorship cases 6—10*

Case	Owner	Joint Owner	Annuitant	Beneficiary	First Death
6	Husband	None	Wife	Child	Husband
7	Husband	None	Child	Husband	Husband
8	Husband	None	Child	Husband	Child*
9	Husband	None	Child	Wife	Husband
10	Husband	Wife	Wife	Husband	Wife*

Case	Contract Disposition	Can Contract Continue?	1099 Issued?
6	Wife may continue contract in deferred status with herself as owner or elect lump sum or annuity option. Cash surrender value is payable.	Yes	No, if wife continues contract.
7	Child must elect lump sum or annuity option. Cash surrender value is payable.	No	Yes
8	Husband must take lump sum or elect an annuity option. Full contract value is payable.	No	Yes
9	Child must elect lump sum or annuity option. Cash surrender value is payable.	No	Yes
10	Husband may continue contract in deferred status or elect lump sum or annuity option. Full contract value is payable.	Yes	No, if husband continues contract.

Case	Federal Income Tax	Federal Estate Tax	Federal Gift Tax
6	All deferred income taxed to wife at time actually paid out of annuity contract.	Full contract value included in husband's estate - marital deduction available.	None
7	All deferred income taxable to child at time actually paid out of contract.	Full contract value included in husband's estate.	None
8	All deferred income taxable to husband at time actually paid out of anuity contract.	None	None
9	All deferred income taxable to child at time actually paid out of contract.	Full contract value included in husband's estate.	None
10	All deferred income taxed to husband at time actually paid out of annuity contract.	Half of contract value included in wife's estate - marital deduction available.	None

*Minimum death benefit provision applies upon death of the annuitant.

Table D.3 *Survivorship cases 11—14*

Case	Owner	Joint Owner	Annuitant	Beneficiary	First Death
11	Husband	Wife	Wife	Child	Husband
12	Husband	Wife	Wife	Child	Wife*
13	Husband	Wife	Husband	Wife	Husband*
14	Husband	Wife	Child	Husband	Husband

Case	Contract Disposition	Can Contract Continue?	1099 Issued?
11	Wife may continue contract in deferred status or elect lump sum or annuity option. Cash surrender value is payable.	Yes	No, if wife continues contract.
12	Child must elect lump sum or annuity option. Full contract value is payable.	No	Yes
13	Wife may continue contract in deferred status or elect lump sum or annuity option. Full contract value is payable.	Yes	No, if wife continues contract.
14	Wife may continue contract in deferred status or elect lump sum or annuity option. Cash surrender value is payable.	Yes	No, if wife continues contract.

Case	Federal Income Tax	Federal Estate Tax	Federal Gift Tax
11	All deferred income taxed to wife at time actually paid out of annuity contract.	Half of contract value included in husband's estate - marital deduction available.	None
12	All deferred income taxed to child at time actually paid out of annuity contract.	Half of contract value included in wife's estate.	Half of contract value constitutes a gift to the child from the husband.
13	All deferred income taxed to wife at time actually paid out of annuity contract.	Half of contract value included in husband's estate - marital deduction available.	None
14	All deferred income taxed to wife at time actually paid out of annuity contract.	Half of contract value included in husband's estate - marital deduction available.	None

*Minimum death benefit provision applies upon death of the annuitant.

Table D.4 *Survivorship cases 15–19*

Case	Owner	Joint Owner	Annuitant	Beneficiary	First Death
15	Husband	Wife	Child	Husband	Child*
16	Husband	Wife	Child	Wife	Child*
17	Husband	Child	Child	Husband	Husband
18	Husband	Child	Child	Husband	Child*
19	Husband	Child	Child	Wife	Husband

Case	Contract Disposition	Can Contract Continue?	1099 Issued?
15	Husband must either take lump sum or elect an annuity option. Full contract value is payable.	No	Yes
16	Wife must either take lump sum or elect an annuity option. Full contract value is payable.	No	Yes
17	Child must take lump sum or elect an annuity option. Cash surrender value is payable.	No	Yes
18	Husband must take lump sum or elect an annuity option. Full contract value is payable.	No	Yes
19	Child must take lump sum or elect an annuity option. Cash surrender value is payable.	No	Yes

Case	Federal Income Tax	Federal Estate Tax	Federal Gift Tax
15	All deferred income taxed to husband at time actually paid out of annuity contract.	None	Half of contract value constitutes a non-taxable gift to the husband from the wife. (IRC Section 2523)
16	All deferred income taxed to wife at time actually paid out of annuity contract.	None	Half of contract value constitutes a non-taxable gift to the wife from the husband. (IRC Section 2523)
17	All deferred income taxed to child at time actually paid out of annuity contract.	Half of contract value included in husband's estate - no marital deduction allowed.	None
18	All deferred income taxed to husband at time actually paid out of annuity contract.	Half of contract value included in child's estate.	None
19	All deferred income taxed to child at time actually paid out of annuity contract.	Half of contract value included in husband's estate - no marital deduction allowed.	None

*Minimum death benefit provision applies upon death of the annuitant.

Table D.5 *Survivorship cases 20–24*

Case	Owner	Joint Owner	Annuitant	Beneficiary	First Death
20	Husband	Child	Child	Wife	Child*
21	Parent	Child	Child	Grandchild	Child*
22	Parent	Child	Child	Grandchild	Parent
23	Parent	None	Child	Grandchild	Parent
24	Adult **A	Adult**B	Adult A	Adult A	Adult B

** A and B are unrelated adults.

Case	Contract Disposition	Can Contract Continue?	1099 Issued?
20	Wife must take lump sum or elect an annuity option. Full contract value is payable.	No	Yes
21	Grandchild must take lump sum or elect annuity option. Full contract value is payable.	No	Yes
22	Child must take lump sum or elect annuity option. Cash surrender value is payable.	No	Yes
23	Child must take lump sum or elect annuity option. Cash surrender value is payable.	No	Yes
24	Adult A must elect a lump sum or annuity option. Cash surrender value is payable.	No	Yes

Case	Federal Income Tax	Federal Estate Tax	Federal Gift Tax
20	All deferred income taxed to wife at time actually paid out of annuity contract.	Half of contract value included in child's estate.	Half of contract value constitutes a non-taxable gift to the wife from the husband. (IRC Section 2523)
21	All deferred income taxed to grandchild at time actually paid out of annuity contract.	Half of contract value included in child's estate.	Half of contract value constitutes a gift to the grandchild from the parent. Generation skipping transfer tax may also apply.
22	All deferred income taxed to child at time actually paid out of annuity contract.	Half of contract value included in parent's estate.	None
23	All deferred income taxed to child at time actually paid out of annuity contract.	Full contract value included in parent's estate.	None
24	All deferred income taxed to Adult A at time actually paid out of annuity contract.	Half of contract value included in Adult B's estate.	None

*Minimum death benefit provision applies upon death of the annuitant.

APPENDIX E

Taxable Versus Tax-Deferred Growth

The tables in this appendix depict what happens when a single $10,000 investment is made in a tax-deferred vehicle such as an annuity, versus the growth rate in an investment with the identical rate of return but subject to current income taxes. The tables show the different results assuming a 6, 8, 10, 12, 14, 16, 18, and 20 percent growth rate. In each of these eight tables, a 5-, 10-, 15-, and 20-year time period is covered.

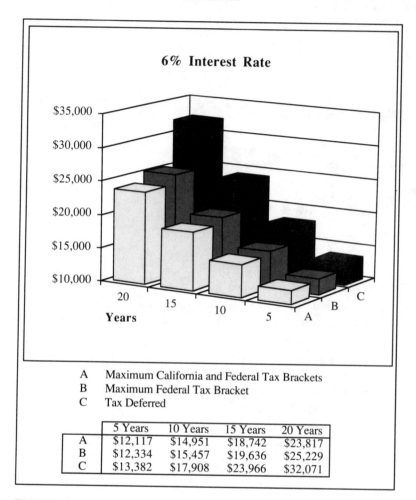

6% Interest Rate

	5 Years	10 Years	15 Years	20 Years
A	$12,117	$14,951	$18,742	$23,817
B	$12,334	$15,457	$19,636	$25,229
C	$13,382	$17,908	$23,966	$32,071

A   Maximum California and Federal Tax Brackets
B   Maximum Federal Tax Bracket
C   Tax Deferred

FIGURE E. 1

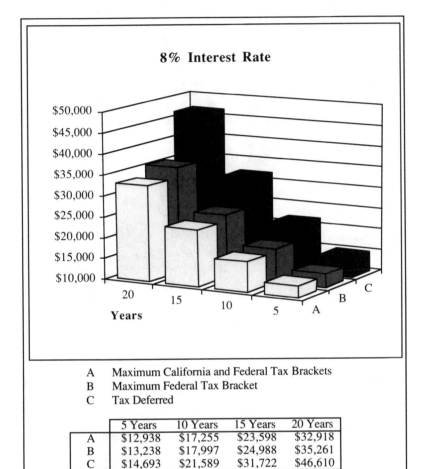

	5 Years	10 Years	15 Years	20 Years
A	$12,938	$17,255	$23,598	$32,918
B	$13,238	$17,997	$24,988	$35,261
C	$14,693	$21,589	$31,722	$46,610

A   Maximum California and Federal Tax Brackets
B   Maximum Federal Tax Bracket
C   Tax Deferred

FIGURE E.2

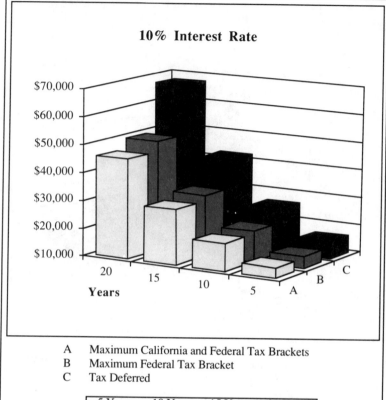

10% Interest Rate

A   Maximum California and Federal Tax Brackets
B   Maximum Federal Tax Bracket
C   Tax Deferred

	5 Years	10 Years	15 Years	20 Years
A	$13,822	$19,977	$29,890	$45,854
B	$14,213	$20,997	$31,923	$49,520
C	$16,105	$25,937	$41,772	$67,275

FIGURE E.3

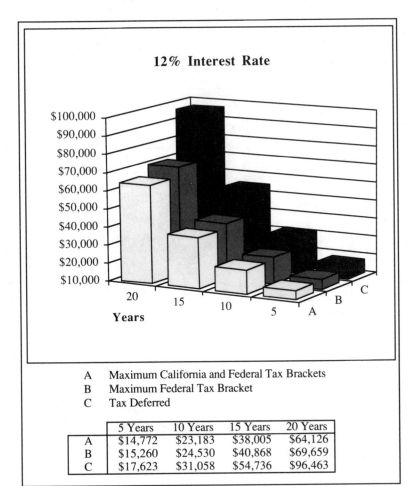

	5 Years	10 Years	15 Years	20 Years
A	$14,772	$23,183	$38,005	$64,126
B	$15,260	$24,530	$40,868	$69,659
C	$17,623	$31,058	$54,736	$96,463

FIGURE E.4

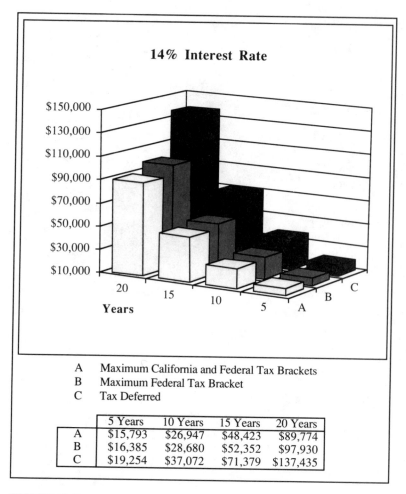

14% Interest Rate

A   Maximum California and Federal Tax Brackets
B   Maximum Federal Tax Bracket
C   Tax Deferred

	5 Years	10 Years	15 Years	20 Years
A	$15,793	$26,947	$48,423	$89,774
B	$16,385	$28,680	$52,352	$97,930
C	$19,254	$37,072	$71,379	$137,435

FIGURE E.5

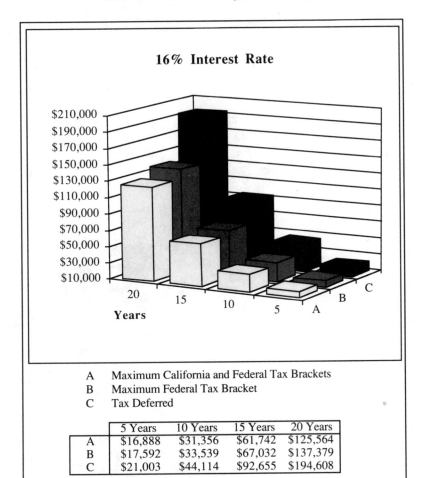

	5 Years	10 Years	15 Years	20 Years
A	$16,888	$31,356	$61,742	$125,564
B	$17,592	$33,539	$67,032	$137,379
C	$21,003	$44,114	$92,655	$194,608

A   Maximum California and Federal Tax Brackets
B   Maximum Federal Tax Bracket
C   Tax Deferred

FIGURE E.6

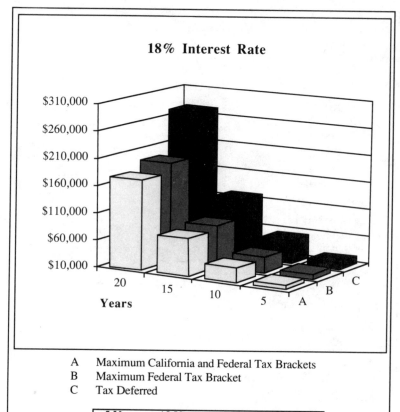

18% Interest Rate

A   Maximum California and Federal Tax Brackets
B   Maximum Federal Tax Bracket
C   Tax Deferred

	5 Years	10 Years	15 Years	20 Years
A	$18,061	$36,504	$78,696	$175,220
B	$18,886	$39,213	$85,719	$192,112
C	$22,878	$52,338	$119,737	$273,930

FIGURE E.7

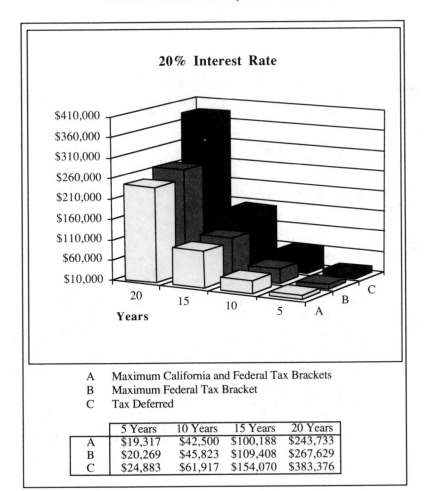

20% Interest Rate

A Maximum California and Federal Tax Brackets
B Maximum Federal Tax Bracket
C Tax Deferred

	5 Years	10 Years	15 Years	20 Years
A	$19,317	$42,500	$100,188	$243,733
B	$20,269	$45,823	$109,408	$267,629
C	$24,883	$61,917	$154,070	$383,376

FIGURE E.8

APPENDIX F

The 50 Largest Insurance Companies

There are close to 2,000 different insurance companies. This appendix shows how the top 125 companies invest their assets.

The pie chart shown in Figure F.1 segregates assets into eight principal categories for the 125 leading life insurance companies. The dollar amount and the percentage of assets in each category are shown. Table F.1 shows the dollar value of assets for the top 50 leading life and health insurers. Almost all of these companies offer annuities.

Total disclosed assets for the 125 leading life and health (L/H) insurers amount to over $1.2 trillion, accounting for over 85% of the industry's total assets. Most insurers continue to invest the bulk of their investments in bonds and mortgages. Combined, the two categories represent 68% of the group's total.

The Biggest Names in Annuity Sales

Annuity sales increased 13% from $114 billion in 1989 to $129 billion in 1990. Figures for 1991 were in the $150 billion range. The top 200 companies accounted for 99% of the total annuity premiums sold in 1991.

Table F.2 lists are the top 10 sellers of individual annuity contracts (group annuity sales to pensions and corporations are considered a different category).

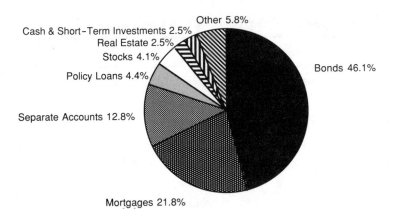

FIGURE F.1 **Asset Distribution for Top 125 L/H Insurers**

Table F.1 *Assets of the Top 50 Companies as of 1991*

Company	*Total Assets*
Prudential Insurance Company of America	129,118,100,000
Metropolitan Life Insurance Company	98,740,300,000
Equitable Life Assurance Soc. U.S.	52,511,914,000
Aetna Life Insurance Company	52,022,600,000
Teachers Insurance & Annuity Assoc. of America	44,374,200,000
New York Life Insurance Company	37,302,400,000
Connecticut General Life Insurance Company	33,991,200,000
Travelers Insurance Company	32,087,500,000
John Hancock Mutual Life Insurance Company	30,924,800,000
Northwestern Mutual Life Insurance Company	28,500,000,000
Massachusetts Mutual Life Insurance Company	28,842,300,000
Principal Mutual Life Insurance Company	24,825,500,000
Manufacturers Life Insurance Company	22,102,500,000
Sun Life Assurance Company of Canada	18,030,900,000
Mutual Life Insurance Company of New York	17,181,300,000
New England Mutual Life Insurance Company	16,666,700,000
Lincoln National Life Insurance Company	16,161,900,000
Great-West Life Assurance Company	15,813,400,000
Confederation Life Insurance Company	15,671,100,000

(continued)

Table F.1 *Assets of the Top 50 Companies as of 1991 (cont.)*

Company	Total Assets
Executive Life Insurance Company	13,168,200,000
IDS Life Insurance Company	13,150,200,000
Mutual Benefit Life Insurance Company	11,601,300,000
Mutual Life Assurance Company of Canada	11,174,900,000
Connecticut Mutual Life Insurance Company	11,133,700,000
Allstate Life Insurance Company	10,994,100,000
Variable Annuity Life Insurance Company	10,857,700,000
State Farm Life Insurance Company	10,839,000,000
Canada Life Assurance Company	10,672,500,000
Nationwide Life Insurance Company	10,451,700,000
Aetna Life Insurance and Annuity Company	9,731,900,000
New York Life Insurance & Annuity Company	9,567,900,000
Equitable Variable Life Insurance Company	8,904,100,000
Pacific Mutual Life Insurance Company	8,630,100,000
Continental Assurance Company	8,586,800,000
Hartford Life Insurance Company	8,238,800,000
Jackson National Life Insurance Company	7,828,700,000
Transamerica Life Insurance & Annuity Co.	7,700,500,000
Crown Life Insurance Company	7,724,800,000
Aid Association for Lutherans	7,127,700,000
Provident National Assurance Company	6,922,200,000
Transamerica Occidental Life Insurance Co.	6,579,800,000
Keystone Provident Life Insurance Company	6,261,000,000
Phoenix Mutual Life Insurance Company	6,162,600,000
State Mutual Life Assurance Company of America	5,609,000,000
Lutheran Brotherhood	5,562,100,000
General American Life Insurance Company	5,550,800,000
Guardian Life Insurance Company of America	5,466,100,000
American Life Insurance Company	5,311,300,000
Penn Mutual Life Insurance Company	5,310,700,000
Kemper Investors Life Insurance Company	5,304,300,000

Table F.2 *Top 10 Sellers of Individual Annuities*

Company Name	Market Share	1990 Sales
Prudential	5.5%	$2.8 billion
Teachers Insurance	5.3%	$2.7 billion
Lincoln National Life	4.6%	$2.4 billion
Jackson National Life	4.0%	$2.1 billion
Allstate Life	3.9%	$2.0 billion
IDS	3.7%	$1.9 billion
Metropolitan Life	2.7%	$1.4 billion
Great Northern	2.6%	$1.3 billion
Fidelity & Guarantee	1.8%	$930 million
Xerox Financial Services Life	1.8%	$920 million

Index

About the Author

Gordon K. Williamson, JD, MBA, MS, CFP, ChFC, RP, is one of the most highly trained investment counselors in the United States. Williamson, a former tax attorney, is a Certified Financial Planner and branch manager of a national brokerage firm. He has been admitted to The Registry of Financial Planning Practitioners, the highest honor one can attain as a financial planner. He holds the two highest designations in the life insurance industry, Chartered Life Underwriter and Chartered Financial Consultant. He is also a real estate broker with an MBA in real estate syndication.

Mr. Williamson is the author of several books, including: *The 100 Best Mutual Funds You Can Buy, The Dearborn Investment Companion, Investment Strategies, Survey of Financial Planning, Tax Shelters, Advanced Investment Vehicles & Techniques, Your Living Trust, Low-Risk Investing,* and *Sooner Than You Think.* He has been the financial editor of various magazines and newspapers and a stock market consultant for a television station.

Gordon K. Williamson & Associates is an investment advisory firm located in La Jolla, California. The firm specializes in financial planning for individuals and institutions of all sizes. Additional information can be obtained by phoning (800) 748-5552 or (619) 454-3938.